I0197092

ENGLISH
NORWEGIAN

THEME-BASED
DICTIONARY

Contains over 5000 commonly
used words

Theme-based dictionary British English-Norwegian - 5000 words
British English collection

By Andrey Taranov

T&P Books vocabularies are intended for helping you learn, memorize and review foreign words. The dictionary is divided into themes, covering all major spheres of everyday activities, business, science, culture, etc.

The process of learning words using T&P Books' theme-based dictionaries gives you the following advantages:

* Correctly grouped source information predetermines success at subsequent stages of word memorization
* Availability of words derived from the same root allowing memorization of word units (rather than separate words)
* Small units of words facilitate the process of establishing associative links needed for consolidation of vocabulary
* Level of language knowledge can be estimated by the number of learned words

T&P Books Publishing
www.tpbooks.com

ISBN: 978-1-78492-017-3

This book is also available in E-book formats.
Please visit www.tpbooks.com or the major online bookstores.

NORWEGIAN THEME-BASED DICTIONARY
British English collection

T&P Books vocabularies are intended to help you learn, memorize, and review foreign words. The vocabulary contains over 5000 commonly used words arranged thematically.

- Vocabulary contains the most commonly used words
- Recommended as an addition to any language course
- Meets the needs of beginners and advanced learners of foreign languages
- Convenient for daily use, revision sessions, and self-testing activities
- Allows you to assess your vocabulary

Special features of the vocabulary

- Words are organized according to their meaning, not alphabetically
- Words are presented in three columns to facilitate the reviewing and self-testing processes
- Words in groups are divided into small blocks to facilitate the learning process
- The vocabulary offers a convenient and simple transcription of each foreign word

The vocabulary has 155 topics including:

Basic Concepts, Numbers, Colors, Months, Seasons, Units of Measurement, Clothing & Accessories, Food & Nutrition, Restaurant, Family Members, Relatives, Character, Feelings, Emotions, Diseases, City, Town, Sightseeing, Shopping, Money, House, Home, Office, Working in the Office, Import & Export, Marketing, Job Search, Sports, Education, Computer, Internet, Tools, Nature, Countries, Nationalities and more ...

TABLE OF CONTENTS

PRONUNCIATION GUIDE

Letter	Norwegian example	T&P phonetic alphabet	English example
Aa	plass	[ɑ], [ɑ:]	bath, to pass
Bb	bøtte, albue	[b]	baby, book
Cc [1]	centimeter	[s]	city, boss
Cc [2]	Canada	[k]	clock, kiss
Dd	radius	[d]	day, doctor
Ee	rett	[e:]	longer than in bell
Ee [3]	begå	[ɛ]	man, bad
Ff	fattig	[f]	face, food
Gg [4]	golf	[g]	game, gold
Gg [5]	gyllen	[j]	yes, New York
Gg [6]	regnbue	[ŋ]	English, ring
Hh	hektar	[h]	humor
Ii	kilometer	[ɪ], [i]	tin, see
Kk	konge	[k]	clock, kiss
Kk [7]	kirke	[h]	humor
Jj	fjerde	[j]	yes, New York
kj	bikkje	[h]	humor
Ll	halvår	[l]	lace, people
Mm	middag	[m]	magic, milk
Nn	november	[n]	name, normal
ng	id_langt	[ŋ]	English, ring
Oo [8]	honning	[ɔ]	bottle, doctor
Oo [9]	fot, krone	[u]	book
Pp	plomme	[p]	pencil, private
Qq	sequoia	[k]	clock, kiss
Rr	sverge	[r]	rice, radio
Ss	appelsin	[s]	city, boss
sk [10]	skikk, skyte	[ʃ]	machine, shark
Tt	stør, torsk	[t]	tourist, trip
Uu	brudd	[y]	fuel, tuna
Vv	kraftverk	[v]	very, river
Ww	webside	[v]	very, river
Xx	mexicaner	[ks]	box, taxi
Yy	nytte	[ɪ], [i]	tin, see
Zz [11]	New Zealand	[s]	star, cats
Ææ	vær, stær	[æ]	chess, man
Øø	ørn, gjø	[ø]	eternal, church
Åå	gås, værhår	[o:]	fall, bomb

9

Comments

[1] before **e, i**
[2] elsewhere
[3] unstressed
[4] before **a, o, u, å**
[5] before **i** and **y**
[6] in combination **gn**
[7] before **i** and **y**
[8] before two consonants
[9] before one consonant
[10] before **i** and **y**
[11] in loanwords only

ABBREVIATIONS
used in the dictionary

English abbreviations

ab.	-	about
adj	-	adjective
adv	-	adverb
anim.	-	animate
as adj	-	attributive noun used as adjective
e.g.	-	for example
etc.	-	et cetera
fam.	-	familiar
fem.	-	feminine
form.	-	formal
inanim.	-	inanimate
masc.	-	masculine
math	-	mathematics
mil.	-	military
n	-	noun
pl	-	plural
pron.	-	pronoun
sb	-	somebody
sing.	-	singular
sth	-	something
v aux	-	auxiliary verb
vi	-	intransitive verb
vi, vt	-	intransitive, transitive verb
vt	-	transitive verb

Norwegian abbreviations

f	-	feminine noun
f pl	-	feminine plural
m	-	masculine noun
m pl	-	masculine plural
m/f	-	masculine, neuter
m/f pl	-	masculine/feminine plural
m/f/n	-	masculine/feminine/neuter
m/n	-	masculine, feminine
n	-	neuter
n pl	-	neuter plural
pl	-	plural

BASIC CONCEPTS

Basic concepts. Part 1

1. Pronouns

I, me	jeg	['jæj]
you	du	[dʉ]
he	han	['hɑn]
she	hun	['hʉn]
it	det, den	['de], ['den]
we	vi	['vi]
you (to a group)	dere	['derə]
they	de	['de]

2. Greetings. Salutations. Farewells

Hello! (fam.)	Hei!	['hæj]
Hello! (form.)	Hallo! God dag!	[hɑ'lʉ], [gʉ 'dɑ]
Good morning!	God morn!	[gʉ 'mɔːn]
Good afternoon!	God dag!	[gʉ'dɑ]
Good evening!	God kveld!	[gʉ 'kvɛl]
to say hello	å hilse	[ɔ 'hilsə]
Hi! (hello)	Hei!	['hæj]
greeting (n)	hilsen (m)	['hilsən]
to greet (vt)	å hilse	[ɔ 'hilsə]
How are you? (form.)	Hvordan står det til?	['vʉːdɑn stoːr de til]
How are you? (fam.)	Hvordan går det?	['vʉːdɑn gor de]
What's new?	Hva nytt?	[va 'nʏt]
Goodbye! (form.)	Ha det bra!	[hɑ de 'brɑ]
Bye! (fam.)	Ha det!	[hɑ 'de]
See you soon!	Vi ses!	[vi sɛs]
Farewell!	Farvel!	[fɑr'vɛl]
to say goodbye	å si farvel	[ɔ 'si fɑr'vɛl]
Cheers!	Ha det!	[hɑ 'de]
Thank you! Cheers!	Takk!	['tɑk]
Thank you very much!	Tusen takk!	['tʉsən tɑk]
My pleasure!	Bare hyggelig	['bɑrə 'hʏgeli]
Don't mention it!	Ikke noe å takke for!	['ikə 'nʉe ɔ 'tɑkə for]
It was nothing	Ingen årsak!	['iŋən 'oːʂɑk]
Excuse me! (fam.)	Unnskyld, ...	['ʉn‚ʂyl ...]
Excuse me! (form.)	Unnskyld meg, ...	['ʉn‚ʂyl me ...]

to excuse (forgive)	å unnskylde	[ɔ 'ʉnˌsylə]
to apologize (vi)	å unnskylde seg	[ɔ 'ʉnˌsylə sæj]
My apologies	Jeg ber om unnskyldning	[jæj ber ɔm 'ʉnˌsyldniŋ]
I'm sorry!	Unnskyld!	['ʉnˌsyl]
to forgive (vt)	å tilgi	[ɔ 'tilˌji]
It's okay! (that's all right)	Ikke noe problem	['ikə 'nʉe prʉ'blem]
please (adv)	vær så snill	['vær sɔ 'snil]

Don't forget!	Ikke glem!	['ikə 'glem]
Certainly!	Selvfølgelig!	[sɛl'følgəli]
Of course not!	Selvfølgelig ikke!	[sɛl'følgəli 'ikə]
Okay! (I agree)	OK! Enig!	[ɔ'kɛj], ['ɛni]
That's enough!	Det er nok!	[de ær 'nɔk]

3. How to address

Excuse me, ...	Unnskyld, ...	['ʉnˌsyl ...]
mister, sir	Herr	['hær]
madam	Fru	['frʉ]
miss	Frøken	['frøkən]
young man	unge mann	['ʉŋə ˌman]
young man (little boy)	guttunge	['gʉtˌʉŋə]
miss (little girl)	frøken	['frøkən]

4. Cardinal numbers. Part 1

0 zero	null	['nʉl]
1 one	en	['en]
2 two	to	['tʉ]
3 three	tre	['tre]
4 four	fire	['fire]

5 five	fem	['fɛm]
6 six	seks	['sɛks]
7 seven	sju	['ʂʉ]
8 eight	åtte	['ɔtə]
9 nine	ni	['ni]

10 ten	ti	['ti]
11 eleven	elleve	['ɛlvə]
12 twelve	tolv	['tɔl]
13 thirteen	tretten	['trɛtən]
14 fourteen	fjorten	['fjɔːʈən]

15 fifteen	femten	['fɛmtən]
16 sixteen	seksten	['sæjstən]
17 seventeen	sytten	['svtən]
18 eighteen	atten	['atən]
19 nineteen	nitten	['nitən]

20 twenty	tjue	['çʉe]
21 twenty-one	tjueen	['çʉe en]

| 22 twenty-two | tjueto | ['çɤe tʊ] |
| 23 twenty-three | tjuetre | ['çɤe tre] |

30 thirty	tretti	['trɛti]
31 thirty-one	trettien	['trɛti en]
32 thirty-two	trettito	['trɛti tʊ]
33 thirty-three	trettitre	['trɛti tre]

40 forty	førti	['fœ:ţi]
41 forty-one	førtien	['fœ:ţi en]
42 forty-two	førtito	['fœ:ţi tʊ]
43 forty-three	førtitre	['fœ:ţi tre]

50 fifty	femti	['fɛmti]
51 fifty-one	femtien	['fɛmti en]
52 fifty-two	femtito	['fɛmti tʊ]
53 fifty-three	femtitre	['fɛmti tre]

60 sixty	seksti	['sɛksti]
61 sixty-one	sekstien	['sɛksti en]
62 sixty-two	sekstito	['sɛksti tʊ]
63 sixty-three	sekstitre	['sɛksti tre]

70 seventy	sytti	['sʏti]
71 seventy-one	syttien	['sʏti en]
72 seventy-two	syttito	['sʏti tʊ]
73 seventy-three	syttitre	['sʏti tre]

80 eighty	åtti	['ɔti]
81 eighty-one	åttien	['ɔti en]
82 eighty-two	åttito	['ɔti tʊ]
83 eighty-three	åttitre	['ɔti tre]

90 ninety	nitti	['niti]
91 ninety-one	nittien	['niti en]
92 ninety-two	nittito	['niti tʊ]
93 ninety-three	nittitre	['niti tre]

5. Cardinal numbers. Part 2

100 one hundred	hundre	['hʉndrə]
200 two hundred	to hundre	['tʊ ˌhʉndrə]
300 three hundred	tre hundre	['tre ˌhʉndrə]
400 four hundred	fire hundre	['fire ˌhʉndrə]
500 five hundred	fem hundre	['fɛm ˌhʉndrə]

600 six hundred	seks hundre	['sɛks ˌhʉndrə]
700 seven hundred	syv hundre	['sʏv ˌhʉndrə]
800 eight hundred	åtte hundre	['ɔtə ˌhʉndrə]
900 nine hundred	ni hundre	['ni ˌhʉndrə]

1000 one thousand	tusen	['tʉsən]
2000 two thousand	to tusen	['tʊ ˌtʉsən]
3000 three thousand	tre tusen	['tre ˌtʉsən]

10000 ten thousand	ti tusen	['ti ˌtʉsən]
one hundred thousand	hundre tusen	['hʉndrə ˌtʉsən]
million	million (m)	[mi'ljun]
billion	milliard (m)	[mi'lja:d]

6. Ordinal numbers

first (adj)	første	['fœʂtə]
second (adj)	annen	['anən]
third (adj)	tredje	['trɛdjə]
fourth (adj)	fjerde	['fjærə]
fifth (adj)	femte	['fɛmtə]

sixth (adj)	sjette	['ʂɛtə]
seventh (adj)	sjuende	['ʂʉenə]
eighth (adj)	åttende	['ɔtenə]
ninth (adj)	niende	['nienə]
tenth (adj)	tiende	['tienə]

7. Numbers. Fractions

fraction	brøk (m)	['brøk]
one half	en halv	[en 'hal]
one third	en tredjedel	[en 'trɛdjəˌdel]
one quarter	en fjerdedel	[en 'fjærəˌdel]

one eighth	en åttendedel	[en 'ɔtenəˌdel]
one tenth	en tiendedel	[en 'tienəˌdel]
two thirds	to tredjedeler	['tʉ 'trɛdjəˌdelər]
three quarters	tre fjerdedeler	['tre 'fjærˌdelər]

8. Numbers. Basic operations

subtraction	subtraksjon (m)	[sʉbtrak'ʂʉn]
to subtract (vi, vt)	å subtrahere	[ɔ 'sʉbtraˌherə]
division	divisjon (m)	[divi'ʂʉn]
to divide (vt)	å dividere	[ɔ divi'derə]

addition	addisjon (m)	[adi'ʂʉn]
to add up (vt)	å addere	[ɔ a'derə]
to add (vi)	å addere	[ɔ a'derə]
multiplication	multiplikasjon (m)	[mʉltiplika'ʂʉn]
to multiply (vt)	å multiplisere	[ɔ mʉltipli'serə]

9. Numbers. Miscellaneous

| digit, figure | siffer (n) | ['sifər] |
| number | tall (n) | ['tal] |

numeral	tallord (n)	['tɑlˌuːr]
minus sign	minus (n)	['minʉs]
plus sign	pluss (n)	['plʉs]
formula	formel (m)	['fɔrməl]

calculation	beregning (m/f)	[beˈrɛjniŋ]
to count (vi, vt)	å telle	[ɔ 'tɛlə]
to count up	å telle opp	[ɔ 'tɛlə ɔp]
to compare (vt)	å sammenlikne	[ɔ 'samənˌliknə]

How much?	Hvor mye?	[vʊr 'mye]
How many?	Hvor mange?	[vʊr 'maŋə]
sum, total	sum (m)	['sʉm]
result	resultat (n)	[resʉl'tɑt]
remainder	rest (m)	['rɛst]

a few (e.g., ~ years ago)	noen	['nʊən]
few (I have ~ friends)	få, ikke mange	['fɔ], ['ikə ˌmaŋə]
a little (~ tired)	lite	['litə]
the rest	rest (m)	['rɛst]
one and a half	halvannen	[hal'anən]
dozen	dusin (n)	[dʉ'sin]

in half (adv)	i 2 halvdeler	[i tʉ hal'delər]
equally (evenly)	jevnt	['jɛvnt]
half	halvdel (m)	['haldel]
time (three ~s)	gang (m)	['gaŋ]

10. The most important verbs. Part 1

to advise (vt)	å råde	[ɔ 'roːdə]
to agree (say yes)	å samtykke	[ɔ 'samˌtʏkə]
to answer (vi, vt)	å svare	[ɔ 'svarə]
to apologize (vi)	å unnskylde seg	[ɔ 'ʉnˌʂylə sæj]
to arrive (vi)	å ankomme	[ɔ 'anˌkɔmə]

to ask (~ oneself)	å spørre	[ɔ 'spørə]
to ask (~ sb to do sth)	å be	[ɔ 'be]
to be (vi)	å være	[ɔ 'værə]

to be afraid	å frykte	[ɔ 'frʏktə]
to be hungry	å være sulten	[ɔ 'værə 'sʉltən]
to be interested in ...	å interessere seg	[ɔ intəre'serə sæj]
to be needed	å være behøv	[ɔ 'værə bə'høv]
to be surprised	å bli forundret	[ɔ 'bli fɔ'rʉndrət]

to be thirsty	å være tørst	[ɔ 'værə 'tœʂt]
to begin (vt)	å begynne	[ɔ be'jinə]
to belong to ...	å tilhøre ...	[ɔ 'tilˌhørə ...]
to boast (vi)	å prale	[ɔ 'pralə]
to break (split into pieces)	å bryte	[ɔ 'brytə]
to call (~ for help)	å tilkalle	[ɔ 'tilˌkalə]
can (v aux)	å kunne	[ɔ 'kʉnə]
to catch (vt)	å fange	[ɔ 'faŋə]

to change (vt)	å endre	[ɔ 'ɛndrə]
to choose (select)	å velge	[ɔ 'vɛlgə]
to come down (the stairs)	å gå ned	[ɔ 'gɔ ne]

to compare (vt)	å sammenlikne	[ɔ 'samən,liknə]
to complain (vi, vt)	å klage	[ɔ 'klagə]
to confuse (mix up)	å forveksle	[ɔ fɔr'vɛkʂlə]
to continue (vt)	å fortsette	[ɔ 'fɔrt,sɛtə]
to control (vt)	å kontrollere	[ɔ kʊntrɔ'lerə]
to cook (dinner)	å lage	[ɔ 'lagə]

to cost (vt)	å koste	[ɔ 'kɔstə]
to count (add up)	å telle	[ɔ 'tɛlə]
to count on ...	å regne med ...	[ɔ 'rɛjnə me ...]
to create (vt)	å opprette	[ɔ 'ɔp,rɛtə]
to cry (weep)	å gråte	[ɔ 'grɔːtə]

11. The most important verbs. Part 2

to deceive (vi, vt)	å fuske	[ɔ 'fʉskə]
to decorate (tree, street)	å pryde	[ɔ 'prydə]
to defend (a country, etc.)	å forsvare	[ɔ fɔ'ʂvarə]
to demand (request firmly)	å kreve	[ɔ 'krevə]
to dig (vt)	å grave	[ɔ 'gravə]

to discuss (vt)	å diskutere	[ɔ diskʉ'terə]
to do (vt)	å gjøre	[ɔ 'jørə]
to doubt (have doubts)	å tvile	[ɔ 'tvilə]
to drop (let fall)	å tappe	[ɔ 'tapə]
to enter (room, house, etc.)	å komme inn	[ɔ 'kɔmə in]

to excuse (forgive)	å unnskylde	[ɔ 'ʉn,ʂylə]
to exist (vi)	å eksistere	[ɔ ɛksi'sterə]
to expect (foresee)	å forutse	[ɔ 'fɔrʉt,se]
to explain (vt)	å forklare	[ɔ fɔr'klarə]
to fall (vi)	å falle	[ɔ 'falə]

to fancy (vt)	å like	[ɔ 'likə]
to find (vt)	å finne	[ɔ 'finə]
to finish (vt)	å slutte	[ɔ 'ʂlʉtə]
to fly (vi)	å fly	[ɔ 'fly]
to follow ... (come after)	å følge etter ...	[ɔ 'følə 'ɛter ...]

to forget (vi, vt)	å glemme	[ɔ 'glemə]
to forgive (vt)	å tilgi	[ɔ 'til,ji]
to give (vt)	å gi	[ɔ 'ji]
to give a hint	å gi et vink	[ɔ 'ji et 'vink]
to go (on foot)	å gå	[ɔ 'gɔ]

to go for a swim	å bade	[ɔ 'badə]
to go out (for dinner, etc.)	å gå ut	[ɔ 'gɔ ʉt]
to guess (the answer)	å gjette	[ɔ 'jɛtə]
to have (vt)	å ha	[ɔ 'ha]
to have breakfast	å spise frokost	[ɔ 'spisə ,frʊkɔst]

to have dinner	å spise middag	[ɔ 'spisə 'mi‚dɑ]
to have lunch	å spise lunsj	[ɔ 'spisə ‚lʉnʂ]
to hear (vt)	å høre	[ɔ 'hørə]

to help (vt)	å hjelpe	[ɔ 'jɛlpə]
to hide (vt)	å gjemme	[ɔ 'jɛmə]
to hope (vi, vt)	å håpe	[ɔ 'hoːpə]
to hunt (vi, vt)	å jage	[ɔ 'jagə]
to hurry (vi)	å skynde seg	[ɔ 'ʂynə sæj]

12. The most important verbs. Part 3

to inform (vt)	å informere	[ɔ infɔr'merə]
to insist (vi, vt)	å insistere	[ɔ insi'sterə]
to insult (vt)	å fornærme	[ɔ fɔː'nærmə]
to invite (vt)	å innby, å invitere	[ɔ 'inby], [ɔ invi'terə]
to joke (vi)	å spøke	[ɔ 'spøkə]

to keep (vt)	å beholde	[ɔ be'hɔlə]
to keep silent	å tie	[ɔ 'tie]
to kill (vt)	å døde, å myrde	[ɔ 'dødə], [ɔ 'mʏːɖə]
to know (sb)	å kjenne	[ɔ 'çɛnə]
to know (sth)	å vite	[ɔ 'vitə]
to laugh (vi)	å le, å skratte	[ɔ 'le], [ɔ 'skratə]

to liberate (city, etc.)	å befri	[ɔ be'fri]
to look for … (search)	å søke …	[ɔ 'søkə …]
to love (sb)	å elske	[ɔ 'ɛlskə]
to make a mistake	å gjøre feil	[ɔ 'jørə ‚fæjl]
to manage, to run	å styre, å lede	[ɔ 'styrə], [ɔ 'ledə]
to mean (signify)	å bety	[ɔ 'bety]
to mention (talk about)	å omtale, å nevne	[ɔ 'ɔm‚talə], [ɔ 'nɛvnə]
to miss (school, etc.)	å skulke	[ɔ 'skʉlkə]
to notice (see)	å bemerke	[ɔ be'mærkə]
to object (vi, vt)	å innvende	[ɔ 'in‚vɛnə]

to observe (see)	å observere	[ɔ ɔbsɛr'verə]
to open (vt)	å åpne	[ɔ 'ɔpnə]
to order (meal, etc.)	å bestille	[ɔ be'stilə]
to order (mil.)	å beordre	[ɔ be'ɔrdrə]
to own (possess)	å besidde, å eie	[ɔ bɛ'sidə], [ɔ 'æje]

to participate (vi)	å delta	[ɔ 'dɛlta]
to pay (vi, vt)	å betale	[ɔ be'talə]
to permit (vt)	å tillate	[ɔ 'ti‚latə]
to plan (vt)	å planlegge	[ɔ 'plan‚legə]
to play (children)	å leke	[ɔ 'lekə]

to pray (vi, vt)	å be	[ɔ 'be]
to prefer (vt)	å foretrekke	[ɔ 'fɔrə‚trɛkə]
to promise (vt)	å love	[ɔ 'lɔvə]
to pronounce (vt)	å uttale	[ɔ 'ʉt‚talə]
to propose (vt)	å foreslå	[ɔ 'fɔrə‚slɔ]
to punish (vt)	å straffe	[ɔ 'strɑfə]

13. The most important verbs. Part 4

to read (vi, vt)	å lese	[ɔ 'lesə]
to recommend (vt)	å anbefale	[ɔ 'ɑnbeˌfɑlə]
to refuse (vi, vt)	å vegre seg	[ɔ 'vɛgrə sæj]
to regret (be sorry)	å beklage	[ɔ be'klɑgə]
to rent (sth from sb)	å leie	[ɔ 'læjə]
to repeat (say again)	å gjenta	[ɔ 'jɛntɑ]
to reserve, to book	å reservere	[ɔ resɛr'verə]
to run (vi)	å løpe	[ɔ 'løpə]
to save (rescue)	å redde	[ɔ 'rɛdə]
to say (~ thank you)	å si	[ɔ 'si]
to scold (vt)	å skjelle	[ɔ 'ʂɛːlə]
to see (vt)	å se	[ɔ 'se]
to sell (vt)	å selge	[ɔ 'sɛlə]
to send (vt)	å sende	[ɔ 'sɛnə]
to shoot (vi)	å skyte	[ɔ 'ʂytə]
to shout (vi)	å skrike	[ɔ 'skrikə]
to show (vt)	å vise	[ɔ 'visə]
to sign (document)	å underskrive	[ɔ 'ʉnəˌskrivə]
to sit down (vi)	å sette seg	[ɔ 'sɛtə sæj]
to smile (vi)	å smile	[ɔ 'smilə]
to speak (vi, vt)	å tale	[ɔ 'tɑlə]
to steal (money, etc.)	å stjele	[ɔ 'stjelə]
to stop (for pause, etc.)	å stoppe	[ɔ 'stɔpə]
to stop (please ~ calling me)	å slutte	[ɔ 'ʂlʉtə]
to study (vt)	å studere	[ɔ stʉ'derə]
to swim (vi)	å svømme	[ɔ 'svœmə]
to take (vt)	å ta	[ɔ 'tɑ]
to think (vi, vt)	å tenke	[ɔ 'tɛnkə]
to threaten (vt)	å true	[ɔ 'trʉe]
to touch (with hands)	å røre	[ɔ 'rørə]
to translate (vt)	å oversette	[ɔ 'ɔvəˌsɛtə]
to trust (vt)	å stole på	[ɔ 'stʉlə pɔ]
to try (attempt)	å prøve	[ɔ 'prøvə]
to turn (e.g., ~ left)	å svinge	[ɔ 'sviŋə]
to underestimate (vt)	å undervurdere	[ɔ 'ʉnərvʉːˌderə]
to understand (vt)	å forstå	[ɔ fɔ'ʂtɔ]
to unite (vt)	å forene	[ɔ fo'renə]
to wait (vt)	å vente	[ɔ 'vɛntə]
to want (wish, desire)	å ville	[ɔ 'vilə]
to warn (vt)	å varsle	[ɔ 'vɑʂlə]
to work (vi)	å arbeide	[ɔ 'ɑrˌbæjdə]
to write (vt)	å skrive	[ɔ 'skrivə]
to write down	å skrive ned	[ɔ 'skrivə ne]

14. Colours

colour	farge (m)	['fɑrgə]
shade (tint)	nyanse (m)	[ny'ɑnse]
hue	fargetone (m)	['fɑrgə͵tʉnə]
rainbow	regnbue (m)	['ræjn͵bʉ:ə]
white (adj)	hvit	['vit]
black (adj)	svart	['svɑ:ʈ]
grey (adj)	grå	['grɔ]
green (adj)	grønn	['grœn]
yellow (adj)	gul	['gʉl]
red (adj)	rød	['rø]
blue (adj)	blå	['blɔ]
light blue (adj)	lyseblå	['lysə͵blɔ]
pink (adj)	rosa	['rɔsɑ]
orange (adj)	oransje	[ɔ'rɑnʂɛ]
violet (adj)	fiolett	[fiʊ'lət]
brown (adj)	brun	['brʉn]
golden (adj)	gullgul	['gʉl]
silvery (adj)	sølv-	['søl-]
beige (adj)	beige	['bɛ:ʂ]
cream (adj)	kremfarget	['krɛm͵fɑrgət]
turquoise (adj)	turkis	[tʉr'kis]
cherry red (adj)	kirsebærrød	['çiʂəbær͵rød]
lilac (adj)	lilla	['lilɑ]
crimson (adj)	karminrød	['kɑrmʊ'sin͵rød]
light (adj)	lys	['lys]
dark (adj)	mørk	['mœrk]
bright, vivid (adj)	klar	['klɑr]
coloured (pencils)	farge-	['fɑrgə-]
colour (e.g. ~ film)	farge-	['fɑrgə-]
black-and-white (adj)	svart-hvit	['svɑ:ʈ vit]
plain (one-coloured)	ensfarget	['ɛns͵fɑrgət]
multicoloured (adj)	mangefarget	['mɑŋə͵fɑrgət]

15. Questions

Who?	Hvem?	['vɛm]
What?	Hva?	['vɑ]
Where? (at, in)	Hvor?	['vʊr]
Where (to)?	Hvorhen?	['vʊrhen]
From where?	Hvorfra?	['vʊrfrɑ]
When?	Når?	[nɔr]
Why? (What for?)	Hvorfor?	['vʊrfʊr]
Why? (~ are you crying?)	Hvorfor?	['vʊrfʊr]
What for?	Hvorfor?	['vʊrfʊr]

How? (in what way)	Hvordan?	['vʊːdɑn]
What? (What kind of ...?)	Hvilken?	['vilkən]
Which?	Hvilken?	['vilkən]

To whom?	Til hvem?	[til 'vɛm]
About whom?	Om hvem?	[ɔm 'vɛm]
About what?	Om hva?	[ɔm 'vɑ]
With whom?	Med hvem?	[me 'vɛm]

How many?	Hvor mange?	[vʊr 'mɑŋə]
How much?	Hvor mye?	[vʊr 'mye]
Whose?	Hvis?	['vis]

16. Prepositions

with (accompanied by)	med	[me]
without	uten	['ʉtən]
to (indicating direction)	til	['til]
about (talking ~ ...)	om	['ɔm]
before (in time)	før	['før]
in front of ...	foran, framfor	['fɔrɑn], ['frɑmfɔr]

under (beneath, below)	under	['ʉnər]
above (over)	over	['ɔvər]
on (atop)	på	['pɔ]
from (off, out of)	fra	['frɑ]
of (made from)	av	[ɑː]

| in (e.g. ~ ten minutes) | om | ['ɔm] |
| over (across the top of) | over | ['ɔvər] |

17. Function words. Adverbs. Part 1

Where? (at, in)	Hvor?	['vʊr]
here (adv)	her	['hɛr]
there (adv)	der	['dɛr]

| somewhere (to be) | et sted | [et 'sted] |
| nowhere (not anywhere) | ingensteds | ['iŋən,stɛts] |

| by (near, beside) | ved | ['ve] |
| by the window | ved vinduet | [ve 'vindʉə] |

Where (to)?	Hvorhen?	['vʊrhen]
here (e.g. come ~!)	hit	['hit]
there (e.g. to go ~)	dit	['dit]
from here (adv)	herfra	['hɛr,frɑ]
from there (adv)	derfra	['dɛr,frɑ]

close (adv)	nær	['nær]
far (adv)	langt	['lɑŋt]
near (e.g. ~ Paris)	nær	['nær]

| nearby (adv) | i nærheten | [i 'nær‚hetən] |
| not far (adv) | ikke langt | ['ikə 'laŋt] |

left (adj)	venstre	['vɛnstrə]
on the left	til venstre	[til 'vɛnstrə]
to the left	til venstre	[til 'vɛnstrə]

right (adj)	høyre	['højrə]
on the right	til høyre	[til 'højrə]
to the right	til høyre	[til 'højrə]

in front (adv)	foran	['foran]
front (as adj)	fremre	['frɛmrə]
ahead (the kids ran ~)	fram	['fram]

behind (adv)	bakom	['bakɔm]
from behind	bakfra	['bak‚fra]
back (towards the rear)	tilbake	[til'bakə]

| middle | midt (m) | ['mit] |
| in the middle | i midten | [i 'mitən] |

at the side	fra siden	[fra 'sidən]
everywhere (adv)	overalt	[ɔvər'alt]
around (in all directions)	rundt omkring	['runt ɔm'kriŋ]

from inside	innofra	['inə‚fra]
somewhere (to go)	et sted	[et 'stɛd]
straight (directly)	rett, direkte	['rɛt], ['di'rɛktə]
back (e.g. come ~)	tilbake	[til'bakə]

| from anywhere | et eller annet steds fra | [et 'elər ‚aːnt 'stɛts fra] |
| from somewhere | et eller annet steds fra | [et 'elər ‚aːnt 'stɛts fra] |

firstly (adv)	for det første	[for de 'fœştə]
secondly (adv)	for det annet	[for de 'aːnt]
thirdly (adv)	for det tredje	[for de 'trɛdje]

suddenly (adv)	plutselig	['plutseli]
at first (in the beginning)	i begynnelsen	[i be'jinəlsən]
for the first time	for første gang	[for 'fœştə ‚gaŋ]
long before ...	lenge før ...	['leŋə 'før ...]
anew (over again)	på nytt	[pɔ 'nʏt]
for good (adv)	for godt	[for 'gɔt]

never (adv)	aldri	['aldri]
again (adv)	igjen	[i'jɛn]
now (adv)	nå	['nɔ]
often (adv)	ofte	['ɔftə]
then (adv)	da	['da]
urgently (quickly)	omgående	['ɔm‚gɔːnə]
usually (adv)	vanligvis	['vanli‚vis]

by the way, ...	forresten, ...	[fɔ'rɛstən ...]
possible (that is ~)	mulig, kanskje	['muli], ['kanşə]
probably (adv)	sannsynligvis	[san'sʏnli‚vis]

maybe (adv)	kanskje	['kanʂə]
besides ...	dessuten, ...	[des'ʉtən ...]
that's why ...	derfor ...	['dɛrfor ...]
in spite of ...	på tross av ...	['pɔ 'trɔs ɑ: ...]
thanks to ...	takket være ...	['takət ˌværə ...]

what (pron.)	hva	['va]
that (conj.)	at	[at]
something	noe	['nʊe]
anything (something)	noe	['nʊe]
nothing	ingenting	['iŋəntiŋ]

who (pron.)	hvem	['vɛm]
someone	noen	['nʊən]
somebody	noen	['nʊən]

nobody	ingen	['iŋən]
nowhere (a voyage to ~)	ingensteds	['iŋənˌstɛts]
nobody's	ingens	['iŋəns]
somebody's	noens	['nʊəns]

so (I'm ~ glad)	så	['sɔ:]
also (as well)	også	['ɔsɔ]
too (as well)	også	['ɔsɔ]

18. Function words. Adverbs. Part 2

Why?	Hvorfor?	['vʊrfʊr]
for some reason	av en eller annen grunn	[ɑ: en elər 'anən ˌgrʉn]
because ...	fordi ...	[fɔ'di ...]
for some purpose	av en eller annen grunn	[ɑ: en elər 'anən ˌgrʉn]

and	og	['ɔ]
or	eller	['elər]
but	men	['men]
for (e.g. ~ me)	for, til	[fɔr], [til]

too (excessively)	for, altfor	['fɔr], ['altfor]
only (exclusively)	bare	['barə]
exactly (adv)	presis, eksakt	[prɛ'sis], [ɛk'sakt]
about (more or less)	cirka	['sirka]

approximately (adv)	omtrent	[ɔm'trɛnt]
approximate (adj)	omtrentlig	[ɔm'trɛntli]
almost (adv)	nesten	['nɛstən]
the rest	rest (m)	['rɛst]

the other (second)	den annen	[den 'anən]
other (different)	andre	['andrə]
each (adj)	hver	['vɛr]
any (no matter which)	hvilken som helst	['vilkən sɔm 'hɛlst]
many, much (a lot of)	mye	['mye]
many people	mange	['maŋə]
all (everyone)	alle	['alə]

in return for ...	til gjengjeld for ...	[til 'jɛnjɛl fɔr ...]
in exchange (adv)	istedenfor	[i'steden,fɔr]
by hand (made)	for hånd	[fɔr 'hɔn]
hardly (negative opinion)	neppe	['nepə]

probably (adv)	sannsynligvis	[sɑn'sʏnli,vis]
on purpose (intentionally)	med vilje	[me 'vilje]
by accident (adv)	tilfeldigvis	[til'fɛldivis]

very (adv)	meget	['megət]
for example (adv)	for eksempel	[fɔr ɛk'sɛmpəl]
between	mellom	['mɛlɔm]
among	blant	['blɑnt]
so much (such a lot)	så mye	['sɔ: mye]
especially (adv)	særlig	['sæ:ˌli]

Basic concepts. Part 2

19. Weekdays

Monday	mandag (m)	['mɑn,dɑ]
Tuesday	tirsdag (m)	['tiʂ,dɑ]
Wednesday	onsdag (m)	['ʉns,dɑ]
Thursday	torsdag (m)	['toʂ,dɑ]
Friday	fredag (m)	['frɛ,dɑ]
Saturday	lørdag (m)	['lør,dɑ]
Sunday	søndag (m)	['søn,dɑ]

today (adv)	i dag	[i 'dɑ]
tomorrow (adv)	i morgen	[i 'mɔ:ən]
the day after tomorrow	i overmorgen	[i 'ɔvər,mɔ:ən]
yesterday (adv)	i går	[i 'gɔr]
the day before yesterday	i forgårs	[i 'fɔr,gɔʂ]

day	dag (m)	['dɑ]
working day	arbeidsdag (m)	['ɑrbæjds,dɑ]
public holiday	festdag (m)	['fɛst,dɑ]
day off	fridag (m)	['fri,dɑ]
weekend	ukeslutt (m), helg (f)	['ʉkə,slʉt], ['hɛlg]

all day long	hele dagen	['helə 'dɑgən]
the next day (adv)	neste dag	['nɛstə ,dɑ]
two days ago	for to dager siden	[fɔr tʉ 'dɑgər ,sidən]
the day before	dagen før	['dɑgən 'før]
daily (adj)	daglig	['dɑgli]
every day (adv)	hver dag	['vɛr dɑ]

week	uke (m/f)	['ʉkə]
last week (adv)	siste uke	['sistə 'ʉkə]
next week (adv)	i neste uke	[i 'nɛstə 'ʉkə]
weekly (adj)	ukentlig	['ʉkəntli]
every week (adv)	hver uke	['vɛr 'ʉkə]
twice a week	to ganger per uke	['tʉ 'gɑŋər per 'ʉkə]
every Tuesday	hver tirsdag	['vɛr 'tiʂdɑ]

20. Hours. Day and night

morning	morgen (m)	['mɔ:ən]
in the morning	om morgenen	[ɔm 'mɔ:enən]
noon, midday	middag (m)	['mi,dɑ]
in the afternoon	om ettermiddagen	[ɔm 'ɛtər,midɑgən]

evening	kveld (m)	['kvɛl]
in the evening	om kvelden	[ɔm 'kvɛlən]

night	natt (m/f)	['nat]
at night	om natta	[ɔm 'nata]
midnight	midnatt (m/f)	['mid‚nat]

second	sekund (m/n)	[se'kʉn]
minute	minutt (n)	[mi'nʉt]
hour	time (m)	['timə]
half an hour	halvtime (m)	['hal‚timə]
a quarter-hour	kvarter (n)	[kva:ʈer]
fifteen minutes	femten minutter	['fɛmtən mi'nʉtər]
24 hours	døgn (n)	['døjn]

sunrise	soloppgang (m)	['sʉlɔp‚gaŋ]
dawn	daggry (n)	['dag‚gry]
early morning	tidlig morgen (m)	['tili 'mɔ:ən]
sunset	solnedgang (m)	['sʉlned‚gaŋ]

early in the morning	tidlig om morgenen	['tili ɔm 'mɔ:enən]
this morning	i morges	[i 'mɔrəs]
tomorrow morning	i morgen tidlig	[i 'mɔ:ən 'tili]

this afternoon	i formiddag	[i 'fɔrmi‚da]
in the afternoon	om ettermiddagen	[ɔm 'ɛtər‚midagən]
tomorrow afternoon	i morgen ettermiddag	[i 'mɔ:ən 'ɛtər‚mida]

tonight (this evening)	i kveld	[i 'kvɛl]
tomorrow night	i morgen kveld	[i 'mɔ:ən ‚kvɛl]

at 3 o'clock sharp	presis klokka tre	[prɛ'sis 'klɔka tre]
about 4 o'clock	ved fire-tiden	[ve 'fire ‚tidən]
by 12 o'clock	innen klokken tolv	['inən 'klɔkən tɔl]

in 20 minutes	om tjue minutter	[ɔm 'çʉe mi'nʉtər]
in an hour	om en time	[ɔm en 'timə]
on time (adv)	i tide	[i 'tidə]

a quarter to …	kvart på …	['kva:ʈ pɔ …]
within an hour	innen en time	['inən en 'timə]
every 15 minutes	hvert kvarter	['vɛ:ʈ kva:'ʈer]
round the clock	døgnet rundt	['døjne ‚rʉnt]

21. Months. Seasons

January	januar (m)	['janʉ‚ar]
February	februar (m)	['febrʉ‚ar]
March	mars (m)	['maʂ]
April	april (m)	[a'pril]
May	mai (m)	['maj]
June	juni (m)	['jʉni]

July	juli (m)	['jʉli]
August	august (m)	[aʊ'gʉst]
September	september (m)	[sep'tɛmbər]
October	oktober (m)	[ɔk'tʉbər]

November	november (m)	[nʊ'vɛmbər]
December	desember (m)	[de'sɛmbər]

spring	vår (m)	['vɔːr]
in spring	om våren	[ɔm 'voːrən]
spring (as adj)	vår-, vårlig	['vɔːr-], ['vɔːli]

summer	sommer (m)	['sɔmər]
in summer	om sommeren	[ɔm 'sɔmerən]
summer (as adj)	sommer-	['sɔmər-]

autumn	høst (m)	['høst]
in autumn	om høsten	[ɔm 'høstən]
autumn (as adj)	høst-, høstlig	['høst-], ['høstli]

winter	vinter (m)	['vintər]
in winter	om vinteren	[ɔm 'vinterən]
winter (as adj)	vinter-	['vintər-]

month	måned (m)	['moːnət]
this month	denne måneden	['dɛnə 'moːnedən]
next month	neste måned	['nɛstə 'moːnət]
last month	forrige måned	['fɔriə ˌmoːnət]

a month ago	for en måned siden	[fɔr en 'moːnət ˌsidən]
in a month (a month later)	om en måned	[ɔm en 'moːnət]
in 2 months (2 months later)	om to måneder	[ɔm 'tʊ 'moːnedər]
the whole month	en hel måned	[en 'hel 'moːnət]
all month long	hele måned	['helə 'moːnət]

monthly (~ magazine)	månedlig	['moːnədli]
monthly (adv)	månedligt	['moːnedlət]
every month	hver måned	[ˌvɛr 'moːnət]
twice a month	to ganger per måned	['tʊ 'ɡaŋər per 'moːnət]

year	år (n)	['ɔr]
this year	i år	[i 'oːr]
next year	neste år	['nɛstə ˌoːr]
last year	i fjor	[i 'fjɔr]

a year ago	for et år siden	[fɔr et 'oːr ˌsidən]
in a year	om et år	[ɔm et 'oːr]
in two years	om to år	[ɔm 'tʊ 'oːr]
the whole year	hele året	['helə 'oːre]
all year long	hele året	['helə 'oːre]

every year	hvert år	['vɛːʈ 'oːr]
annual (adj)	årlig	['oːli]
annually (adv)	årlig, hvert år	['oːli], ['vɛːʈ 'ɔr]
4 times a year	fire ganger per år	['fire 'ɡaŋər per 'oːr]

date (e.g. today's ~)	dato (m)	['datʊ]
date (e.g. ~ of birth)	dato (m)	['datʊ]
calendar	kalender (m)	[ka'lendər]
half a year	halvår (n)	['halˌoːr]
six months	halvår (n)	['halˌoːr]

| season (summer, etc.) | årstid (m/f) | ['oːʂˌtid] |
| century | århundre (n) | ['ɔrˌhʉndrə] |

22. Units of measurement

weight	vekt (m)	['vɛkt]
length	lengde (m/f)	['leŋdə]
width	bredde (m)	['brɛdə]
height	høyde (m)	['højdə]
depth	dybde (m)	['dybdə]
volume	volum (n)	[vɔ'lʉm]
area	areal (n)	[ˌare'al]

gram	gram (n)	['gram]
milligram	milligram (n)	['miliˌgram]
kilogram	kilogram (n)	['çiluˌgram]
ton	tonn (m/n)	['tɔn]
pound	pund (n)	['pʉn]
ounce	unse (m)	['ʉnsə]

metre	meter (m)	['metər]
millimetre	millimeter (m)	['miliˌmetər]
centimetre	centimeter (m)	['sɛntiˌmetər]
kilometre	kilometer (m)	['çiluˌmetər]
mile	mil (m/f)	['mil]

inch	tomme (m)	['tɔmə]
foot	fot (m)	['fʊt]
yard	yard (m)	['jaːrd]

| square metre | kvadratmeter (m) | [kva'dratˌmetər] |
| hectare | hektar (n) | ['hɛktar] |

litre	liter (m)	['litər]
degree	grad (m)	['grad]
volt	volt (m)	['vɔlt]
ampere	ampere (m)	[am'pɛr]
horsepower	hestekraft (m/f)	['hɛstəˌkraft]

quantity	mengde (m)	['mɛŋdə]
a little bit of ...	få ...	['fɔ ...]
half	halvdel (m)	['haldel]

| dozen | dusin (n) | [dʉ'sin] |
| piece (item) | stykke (n) | ['stʏkə] |

| size | størrelse (m) | ['stœrəlsə] |
| scale (map ~) | målestokk (m) | ['moːləˌstɔk] |

minimal (adj)	minimal	[mini'mal]
the smallest (adj)	minste	['minstə]
medium (adj)	middel-	['midəl-]
maximal (adj)	maksimal	[maksi'mal]
the largest (adj)	største	['stœʂtə]

23. Containers

canning jar (glass ~)	glaskrukke (m/f)	['glɑsˌkrʉkə]
tin, can	boks (m)	['bɔks]
bucket	bøtte (m/f)	['bœtə]
barrel	tønne (m)	['tœnə]

wash basin (e.g., plastic ~)	vaskefat (n)	['vɑskəˌfɑt]
tank (100L water ~)	tank (m)	['tɑnk]
hip flask	lommelerke (m/f)	['lʊməˌlærkə]
jerrycan	bensinkanne (m/f)	[bɛn'sinˌkɑnə]
tank (e.g., tank car)	tank (m)	['tɑnk]

mug	krus (n)	['krʉs]
cup (of coffee, etc.)	kopp (m)	['kɔp]
saucer	tefat (n)	['teˌfɑt]
glass (tumbler)	glass (n)	['glɑs]
wine glass	vinglass (n)	['vinˌglɑs]
stock pot (soup pot)	gryte (m/f)	['grytə]

bottle (~ of wine)	flaske (m)	['flɑskə]
neck (of the bottle, etc.)	flaskehals (m)	['flɑskəˌhɑls]

carafe (decanter)	karaffel (m)	[kɑ'rɑfəl]
pitcher	mugge (m/f)	['mʉgə]
vessel (container)	beholder (m)	[be'hɔlər]
pot (crock, stoneware ~)	pott, potte (m)	['pɔt], ['pɔtə]
vase	vase (m)	['vɑsə]

bottle (perfume ~)	flakong (m)	[flɑ'kɔŋ]
vial, small bottle	flaske (m/f)	['flɑskə]
tube (of toothpaste)	tube (m)	['tʉbə]

sack (bag)	sekk (m)	['sɛk]
bag (paper ~, plastic ~)	pose (m)	['pʉsə]
packet (of cigarettes, etc.)	pakke (m/f)	['pɑkə]

box (e.g. shoebox)	eske (m/f)	['ɛskə]
crate	kasse (m/f)	['kɑsə]
basket	kurv (m)	['kʉrv]

HUMAN BEING

Human being. The body

24. Head

head	hode (n)	['hʊdə]
face	ansikt (n)	['ansikt]
nose	nese (m/f)	['nese]
mouth	munn (m)	['mʉn]
eye	øye (n)	['øjə]
eyes	øyne (n pl)	['øjnə]
pupil	pupill (m)	[pʉ'pil]
eyebrow	øyenbryn (n)	['øjən,bryn]
eyelash	øyenvipp (m)	['øjən,vip]
eyelid	øyelokk (m)	['øjə,lɔk]
tongue	tunge (m/f)	['tʉŋə]
tooth	tann (m/f)	['tan]
lips	lepper (m/f pl)	['lepər]
cheekbones	kinnbein (n pl)	['çin,bæjn]
gum	tannkjøtt (n)	['tan,çœt]
palate	gane (m)	['ganə]
nostrils	nesebor (n pl)	['nesə,bʊr]
chin	hake (m/f)	['hakə]
jaw	kjeve (m)	['çɛvə]
cheek	kinn (n)	['çin]
forehead	panne (m/f)	['panə]
temple	tinning (m)	['tiniŋ]
ear	øre (n)	['ørə]
back of the head	bakhode (n)	['bak,hodə]
neck	hals (m)	['hals]
throat	strupe, hals (m)	['strʉpə], ['hals]
hair	hår (n pl)	['hɔr]
hairstyle	frisyre (m)	[fri'syrə]
haircut	hårfasong (m)	['hoːrfa,sɔŋ]
wig	parykk (m)	[pa'rʏk]
moustache	mustasje (m)	[mʉ'staʂə]
beard	skjegg (n)	['ʂɛg]
to have (a beard, etc.)	å ha	[ɔ 'ha]
plait	flette (m/f)	['fletə]
sideboards	bakkenbarter (pl)	['bakən,baːʈər]
red-haired (adj)	rødhåret	['rø,hoːrət]
grey (hair)	grå	['grɔ]

| bald (adj) | skallet | ['skɑlət] |
| bald patch | skallet flekk (m) | ['skɑlət ˌflek] |

| ponytail | hestehale (m) | ['hɛstəˌhɑlə] |
| fringe | pannelugg (m) | ['pɑnəˌlʉg] |

25. Human body

| hand | hånd (m/f) | ['hɔn] |
| arm | arm (m) | ['ɑrm] |

finger	finger (m)	['fiŋər]
toe	tå (m/f)	['tɔ]
thumb	tommel (m)	['tɔməl]
little finger	lillefinger (m)	['liləˌfiŋər]
nail	negl (m)	['nɛjl]

fist	knyttneve (m)	['knʏtˌnevə]
palm	håndflate (m/f)	['hɔnˌflɑtə]
wrist	håndledd (n)	['hɔnˌled]
forearm	underarm (m)	['ʉnərˌɑrm]
elbow	albue (m)	['ɑlˌbʉe]
shoulder	skulder (m)	['skʉldər]

leg	bein (n)	['bæjn]
foot	fot (m)	['fʊt]
knee	kne (n)	['knɛ]
calf (part of leg)	legg (m)	['leg]
hip	hofte (m)	['hɔftə]
heel	hæl (m)	['hæl]

body	kropp (m)	['krɔp]
stomach	mage (m)	['mɑgə]
chest	bryst (n)	['brʏst]
breast	bryst (n)	['brʏst]
flank	side (m/f)	['sidə]
back	rygg (m)	['rʏg]
lower back	korsrygg (m)	['kɔːʂˌrʏg]
waist	liv (n), midje (m/f)	['liv], ['midjə]

navel (belly button)	navle (m)	['nɑvlə]
buttocks	rumpeballer (m pl)	['rʉmpəˌbɑlər]
bottom	bak (m)	['bɑk]

beauty spot	føflekk (m)	['føˌflek]
birthmark (café au lait spot)	fødselsmerke (n)	['føtsəlsˌmærke]
tattoo	tatovering (m/f)	[tatʉ'vɛriŋ]
scar	arr (n)	['ɑr]

Clothing & Accessories

26. Outerwear. Coats

clothes	klær (n)	['klær]
outerwear	yttertøy (n)	['ytə‚tøj]
winter clothing	vinterklær (n pl)	['vintər‚klær]
coat (overcoat)	frakk (m), kåpe (m/f)	['frɑk], ['kɔ:pə]
fur coat	pels (m), pelskåpe (m/f)	['pɛls], ['pɛls‚kɔ:pə]
fur jacket	pelsjakke (m/f)	['pɛls‚jakə]
down coat	dunjakke (m/f)	['dʉn‚jakə]
jacket (e.g. leather ~)	jakke (m/f)	['jakə]
raincoat (trenchcoat, etc.)	regnfrakk (m)	['ræjn‚frɑk]
waterproof (adj)	vanntett	['vɑn‚tɛt]

27. Men's & women's clothing

shirt (button shirt)	skjorte (m/f)	['ʂɔɛ:ʈə]
trousers	bukse (m)	['bʉksə]
jeans	jeans (m)	['dʒins]
suit jacket	dressjakke (m/f)	['drɛs‚jakə]
suit	dress (m)	['drɛs]
dress (frock)	kjole (m)	['çulə]
skirt	skjørt (n)	['ʂø:t]
blouse	bluse (m)	['blʉsə]
knitted jacket (cardigan, etc.)	strikket trøye (m/f)	['strikə 'trøjə]
jacket (of woman's suit)	blazer (m)	['blæsər]
T-shirt	T-skjorte (m/f)	['te‚ʂɔɛ:ʈə]
shorts (short trousers)	shorts (m)	['ʂɔ:ts]
tracksuit	treningsdrakt (m/f)	['treniŋs‚drɑkt]
bathrobe	badekåpe (m/f)	['bɑdə‚kɔ:pə]
pyjamas	pyjamas (m)	[py'ʂɑmɑs]
jumper (sweater)	sweater (m)	['svɛtər]
pullover	pullover (m)	[pʉ'lɔvər]
waistcoat	vest (m)	['vɛst]
tailcoat	livkjole (m)	['liv‚çulə]
dinner suit	smoking (m)	['smɔkiŋ]
uniform	uniform (m)	[ʉni'fɔrm]
workwear	arbeidsklær (n pl)	['ɑrbæjds‚klær]
boiler suit	kjeledress, overall (m)	['çelə‚drɛs], ['ovɛr‚ɔl]
coat (e.g. doctor's smock)	kittel (m)	['çitəl]

28. Clothing. Underwear

underwear	undertøy (n)	['ʉnəˌtøj]
pants	underbukse (m/f)	['ʉnərˌbʉksə]
panties	truse (m/f)	['trʉsə]
vest (singlet)	undertrøye (m/f)	['ʉnəˌtrøjə]
socks	sokker (m pl)	['sɔkər]
nightgown	nattkjole (m)	['natˌçʉlə]
bra	behå (m)	['beˌhɔ]
knee highs (knee-high socks)	knestrømper (m/f pl)	['knɛˌstrømpər]
tights	strømpebukse (m/f)	['strømpəˌbʉksə]
stockings (hold ups)	strømper (m/f pl)	['strømpər]
swimsuit, bikini	badedrakt (m/f)	['badəˌdrɑkt]

29. Headwear

hat	hatt (m)	['hat]
trilby hat	hatt (m)	['hat]
baseball cap	baseball cap (m)	['bɛjsbɔl kɛp]
flatcap	sikspens (m)	['sikspens]
beret	alpelue, baskerlue (m/f)	['alpəˌlʉə], ['baskəˌlʉə]
hood	hette (m/f)	['hɛtə]
panama hat	panamahatt (m)	['panamaˌhat]
knit cap (knitted hat)	strikket lue (m/f)	['strikəˌlʉə]
headscarf	skaut (n)	['skaʉt]
women's hat	hatt (m)	['hat]
hard hat	hjelm (m)	['jɛlm]
forage cap	båtlue (m/f)	['bɔtˌlʉə]
helmet	hjelm (m)	['jɛlm]
bowler	bowlerhatt, skalk (m)	['boʉlerˌhat], ['skɑlk]
top hat	flosshatt (m)	['flɔsˌhat]

30. Footwear

footwear	skotøy (n)	['skʉtøj]
shoes (men's shoes)	skor (m pl)	['skʉr]
shoes (women's shoes)	pumps (m pl)	['pʉmps]
boots (e.g., cowboy ~)	støvler (m pl)	['støvlər]
carpet slippers	tøfler (m pl)	['tøflər]
trainers	tennissko (m pl)	['tɛnisˌskʉ]
trainers	canvas sko (m pl)	['kɑnvas ˌskʉ]
sandals	sandaler (m pl)	[san'dalər]
cobbler (shoe repairer)	skomaker (m)	['skʉˌmakər]
heel	hæl (m)	['hæl]

pair (of shoes)	par (n)	['pɑr]
lace (shoelace)	skolisse (m/f)	['skʉˌlisə]
to lace up (vt)	å snøre	[ɔ 'snørə]
shoehorn	skohorn (n)	['skʉˌhuːŋ]
shoe polish	skokrem (m)	['skʉˌkrɛm]

31. Personal accessories

gloves	hansker (m pl)	['hɑnskər]
mittens	votter (m pl)	['vɔtər]
scarf (muffler)	skjerf (n)	['ʂæərf]

glasses	briller (m pl)	['brilər]
frame (eyeglass ~)	innfatning (m/f)	['inˌfɑtniŋ]
umbrella	paraply (m)	[pɑrɑ'ply]
walking stick	stokk (m)	['stɔk]
hairbrush	hårbørste (m)	['hɔrˌbœʂtə]
fan	vifte (m/f)	['viftə]

tie (necktie)	slips (n)	['slips]
bow tie	sløyfe (m/f)	['ʂløjfə]
braces	bukseseler (m pl)	['bʉksə'selər]
handkerchief	lommetørkle (n)	['lʉməˌtœrklə]

comb	kam (m)	['kɑm]
hair slide	hårspenne (m/f/n)	['hoːrˌspɛnə]
hairpin	hårnål (m/f)	['hoːrˌnol]
buckle	spenne (m/f/n)	['spɛnə]

| belt | belte (m) | ['bɛltə] |
| shoulder strap | skulderreim, rem (m/f) | ['skʉldəˌræjm], ['rem] |

bag (handbag)	veske (m/f)	['vɛskə]
handbag	håndveske (m/f)	['hɔnˌvɛskə]
rucksack	ryggsekk (m)	['rʏgˌsɛk]

32. Clothing. Miscellaneous

fashion	mote (m)	['mʉtə]
in vogue (adj)	moteriktig	['mʉtəˌrikti]
fashion designer	moteskaper (m)	['mʉtəˌskɑpər]

collar	krage (m)	['krɑgə]
pocket	lomme (m/f)	['lʉmə]
pocket (as adj)	lomme-	['lʉmə-]
sleeve	erme (n)	['ærmə]
hanging loop	hempe (m)	['hɛmpə]
flies (on trousers)	gylf, buksesmekk (m)	['gylf], ['bʉksəˌsmɛk]

zip (fastener)	glidelås (m/n)	['glidəˌlos]
fastener	hekte (m/f), knepping (m)	['hɛktə], ['knɛpiŋ]
button	knapp (m)	['knɑp]

| buttonhole | klapphull (n) | ['klɑpˌhʉl] |
| to come off (ab. button) | å falle av | [ɔ 'fɑlə ɑ:] |

to sew (vi, vt)	å sy	[ɔ 'sy]
to embroider (vi, vt)	å brodere	[ɔ brʉ'derə]
embroidery	broderi (n)	[brʉde'ri]
sewing needle	synål (m/f)	['syˌnɔl]
thread	tråd (m)	['trɔ]
seam	søm (m)	['søm]

to get dirty (vi)	å skitne seg til	[ɔ 'şitnə sæj til]
stain (mark, spot)	flekk (m)	['flek]
to crease, crumple (vi)	å bli skrukkete	[ɔ 'bli 'skrʉketə]
to tear, to rip (vt)	å rive	[ɔ 'rivə]
clothes moth	møll (m/n)	['møl]

33. Personal care. Cosmetics

toothpaste	tannpasta (m)	['tanˌpasta]
toothbrush	tannbørste (m)	['tanˌbœştə]
to clean one's teeth	å pusse tennene	[ɔ 'pʉsə 'tɛnənə]

razor	høvel (m)	['høvəl]
shaving cream	barberkrem (m)	[bar'bɛrˌkrɛm]
to shave (vi)	å barbere seg	[ɔ bar'berə sæj]

| soap | såpe (m/f) | ['so:pə] |
| shampoo | sjampo (m) | ['şamˌpʉ] |

scissors	saks (m/f)	['saks]
nail file	neglefil (m/f)	['nɛjləˌfil]
nail clippers	negleklipper (m)	['nɛjləˌklipər]
tweezers	pinsett (m)	[pin'sɛt]

cosmetics	kosmetikk (m)	[kʉsme'tik]
face mask	ansiktsmaske (m/f)	['ansiktsˌmaskə]
manicure	manikyr (m)	[mani'kyr]
to have a manicure	å få manikyr	[ɔ 'fɔ mani'kyr]
pedicure	pedikyr (m)	[pedi'kyr]

make-up bag	sminkeveske (m/f)	['sminkəˌvɛskə]
face powder	pudder (n)	['pʉdər]
powder compact	pudderdåse (m)	['pʉdərˌdo:sə]
blusher	rouge (m)	['ru:ş]

perfume (bottled)	parfyme (m)	[par'fymə]
toilet water (lotion)	eau de toilette (m)	['ɔ: də twa'let]
lotion	lotion (m)	['loʉşɛn]
cologne	eau de cologne (m)	['ɔ: də kɔ'lɔŋ]

eyeshadow	øyeskygge (m)	['øjəˌşygə]
eyeliner	eyeliner (m)	['a:jˌlɑjnər]
mascara	maskara (m)	[ma'skara]
lipstick	leppestift (m)	['lepəˌstift]

nail polish	neglelakk (m)	['nɛjlə,lak]
hair spray	hårlakk (m)	['hoːr,lak]
deodorant	deodorant (m)	[deudʉ'rant]

cream	krem (m)	['krɛm]
face cream	ansiktskrem (m)	['ansikts,krɛm]
hand cream	håndkrem (m)	['hɔn,krɛm]
anti-wrinkle cream	antirynkekrem (m)	[anti'rʏnkə,krɛm]
day cream	dagkrem (m)	['dag,krɛm]
night cream	nattkrem (m)	['nat,krɛm]
day (as adj)	dag-	['dag-]
night (as adj)	natt-	['nat-]

tampon	tampong (m)	[tam'pɔŋ]
toilet paper (toilet roll)	toalettpapir (n)	[tʊa'let pa'pir]
hair dryer	hårføner (m)	['hoːr,fønər]

34. Watches. Clocks

watch (wristwatch)	armbåndsur (n)	['armbɔns,ʉr]
dial	urskive (m/f)	['ʉː,ʂivə]
hand (of clock, watch)	viser (m)	['visər]
metal bracelet	armbånd (n)	['arm,bɔn]
watch strap	rem (m/f)	['rem]

battery	batteri (n)	[batɛ'ri]
to be flat (battery)	å bli utladet	[ɔ 'bli 'ʉt,ladət]
to change a battery	å skifte batteriene	[ɔ 'ʂiftə batɛ'riene]
to run fast	å gå for fort	[ɔ 'gɔ fɔ 'fɔːt]
to run slow	å gå for sakte	[ɔ 'gɔ fɔ 'saktə]

wall clock	veggur (n)	['vɛg,ʉr]
hourglass	timeglass (n)	['timə,glas]
sundial	solur (n)	['sʊl,ʉr]
alarm clock	vekkerklokka (m/f)	['vɛkər,klɔka]
watchmaker	urmaker (m)	['ʉr,makər]
to repair (vt)	å reparere	[ɔ repa'rerə]

Food. Nutricion

35. Food

meat	kjøtt (n)	['çœt]
chicken	høne (m/f)	['hønə]
poussin	kylling (m)	['çyliŋ]
duck	and (m/f)	['an]
goose	gås (m/f)	['gɔs]
game	vilt (n)	['vilt]
turkey	kalkun (m)	[kɑl'kʉn]

pork	svinekjøtt (n)	['svinə,çœt]
veal	kalvekjøtt (n)	['kalvə,çœt]
lamb	fårekjøtt (n)	['fo:rə,çœt]
beef	oksekjøtt (n)	['ɔksə,çœt]
rabbit	kanin (m)	[kɑ'nin]

sausage (bologna, pepperoni, etc.)	pølse (m/f)	['pølsə]
vienna sausage (frankfurter)	wienerpølse (m/f)	['vinər,pølsə]
bacon	bacon (n)	['bɛjkən]
ham	skinke (m)	['şinkə]
gammon	skinke (m)	['şinkə]

pâté	pate, paté (m)	[pɑ'te]
liver	lever (m)	['levər]
mince (minced meat)	kjøttfarse (m)	['çœt,farşə]
tongue	tunge (m/f)	['tʉŋə]

egg	egg (n)	['ɛg]
eggs	egg (n pl)	['ɛg]
egg white	eggehvite (m)	['ɛgə,vitə]
egg yolk	plomme (m/f)	['plʉmə]

fish	fisk (m)	['fisk]
seafood	sjømat (m)	['şø,mat]
crustaceans	krepsdyr (n pl)	['krɛps,dyr]
caviar	kaviar (m)	['kɑvi,ar]

crab	krabbe (m)	['krabə]
prawn	reke (m/f)	['rekə]
oyster	østers (m)	['østəş]
spiny lobster	langust (m)	[lɑŋ'gʉst]
octopus	blekksprut (m)	['blek,sprʉt]
squid	blekksprut (m)	['blek,sprʉt]

sturgeon	stør (m)	['stør]
salmon	laks (m)	['lɑks]
halibut	kveite (m/f)	['kvæjtə]

cod	torsk (m)	['tɔṣk]
mackerel	makrell (m)	[ma'krɛl]
tuna	tunfisk (m)	['tʉnˌfisk]
eel	ål (m)	['ɔl]

trout	ørret (m)	['øret]
sardine	sardin (m)	[sɑ:'din]
pike	gjedde (m/f)	['jɛdə]
herring	sild (m/f)	['sil]

bread	brød (n)	['brø]
cheese	ost (m)	['ʊst]
sugar	sukker (n)	['sʉkər]
salt	salt (n)	['salt]
rice	ris (m)	['ris]
pasta (macaroni)	pasta, makaroni (m)	['pɑstɑ], [mɑkɑ'rʊni]
noodles	nudler (m pl)	['nʉdlər]

butter	smør (n)	['smør]
vegetable oil	vegetabilsk olje (m)	[vegetɑ'bilsk ˌɔljə]
sunflower oil	solsikkeolje (m)	['sʊlsikəˌɔljə]
margarine	margarin (m)	[mɑrgɑ'rin]

| olives | olivener (m pl) | [ʊ'livenər] |
| olive oil | olivenolje (m) | [ʊ'livənˌɔljə] |

milk	melk (m/f)	['mɛlk]
condensed milk	kondensert melk (m/f)	[kʊndən'se:ţ ˌmɛlk]
yogurt	jogurt (m)	['jɔgʉ:t]
soured cream	rømme, syrnet fløte (m)	['rœmə], ['sy:ŋet 'fløtə]
cream (of milk)	fløte (m)	['fløtə]

| mayonnaise | majones (m) | [mɑjɔ'nɛs] |
| buttercream | krem (m) | ['krɛm] |

cereal grains (wheat, etc.)	gryn (n)	['gryn]
flour	mel (n)	['mel]
tinned food	hermetikk (m)	[hɛrme'tik]

cornflakes	cornflakes (m)	['kɔ:ɳflejks]
honey	honning (m)	['hɔniŋ]
jam	syltetøy (n)	['syltəˌtøj]
chewing gum	tyggegummi (m)	['tygəˌgʉmi]

36. Drinks

water	vann (n)	['vɑn]
drinking water	drikkevann (n)	['drikəˌvɑn]
mineral water	mineralvann (n)	[minə'rɑlˌvɑn]

still (adj)	uten kullsyre	['ʉtən kʉl'syrə]
carbonated (adj)	kullsyret	[kʉl'syrət]
sparkling (adj)	med kullsyre	[me kʉl'syrə]
ice	is (m)	['is]

with ice	med is	[me 'is]
non-alcoholic (adj)	alkoholfri	['alkʊhʊlˌfri]
soft drink	alkoholfri drikk (m)	['alkʊhʊlˌfri drik]
refreshing drink	leskedrikk (m)	['leskeˌdrik]
lemonade	limonade (m)	[limɔ'nadə]
spirits	rusdrikker (m pl)	['rʉsˌdrikər]
wine	vin (m)	['vin]
white wine	hvitvin (m)	['vitˌvin]
red wine	rødvin (m)	['røˌvin]
liqueur	likør (m)	[li'kør]
champagne	champagne (m)	[ʂam'panjə]
vermouth	vermut (m)	['værmʉt]
whisky	whisky (m)	['viski]
vodka	vodka (m)	['vɔdka]
gin	gin (m)	['dʒin]
cognac	konjakk (m)	['kʊnjak]
rum	rom (m)	['rʊm]
coffee	kaffe (m)	['kafə]
black coffee	svart kaffe (m)	['svaːʈ 'kafə]
white coffee	kaffe (m) med melk	['kafe me 'mɛlk]
cappuccino	cappuccino (m)	[kapʊ'tʃinɔ]
instant coffee	pulverkaffe (m)	['pʉlvərˌkafə]
milk	melk (m/f)	['mɛlk]
cocktail	cocktail (m)	['kɔkˌtɛjl]
milkshake	milkshake (m)	['milkˌʂɛjk]
juice	jus, juice (m)	['dʒʉs]
tomato juice	tomatjuice (m)	[tʊ'matˌdʒʉs]
orange juice	appelsinjuice (m)	[apel'sinˌdʒʉs]
freshly squeezed juice	nypresset juice (m)	['nyˌprɛsə 'dʒʉs]
beer	øl (m/n)	['øl]
lager	lettøl (n)	['letˌøl]
bitter	mørkt øl (n)	['mœrktˌøl]
tea	te (m)	['te]
black tea	svart te (m)	['svaːʈ ˌte]
green tea	grønn te (m)	['grœn ˌte]

37. Vegetables

vegetables	grønnsaker (m pl)	['grœnˌsakər]
greens	grønnsaker (m pl)	['grœnˌsakər]
tomato	tomat (m)	[tʊ'mat]
cucumber	agurk (m)	[a'gʉrk]
carrot	gulrot (m/f)	['gʉlˌrʊt]
potato	potet (m/f)	[pʊ'tet]
onion	løk (m)	['løk]

garlic	hvitløk (m)	['vit‚løk]
cabbage	kål (m)	['kɔl]
cauliflower	blomkål (m)	['blɔm‚kɔl]
Brussels sprouts	rosenkål (m)	['rʉsən‚kɔl]
broccoli	brokkoli (m)	['brɔkɔli]

beetroot	rødbete (m/f)	['rø‚betə]
aubergine	aubergine (m)	[ɔbɛr'ʂin]
courgette	squash (m)	['skvɔʂ]
pumpkin	gresskar (n)	['grɛskar]
turnip	nepe (m/f)	['nepə]

parsley	persille (m/f)	[pæ'ʂilə]
dill	dill (m)	['dil]
lettuce	salat (m)	[sɑ'lɑt]
celery	selleri (m/n)	[sɛle‚ri]
asparagus	asparges (m)	[ɑ'sparʂəs]
spinach	spinat (m)	[spi'nɑt]

pea	erter (m pl)	['æːtər]
beans	bønner (m/f pl)	['bœnər]
maize	mais (m)	['mais]
kidney bean	bønne (m/f)	['bœnə]

sweet paper	pepper (m)	['pɛpər]
radish	reddik (m)	['rɛdik]
artichoke	artisjokk (m)	[‚ɑːʈi'ʂɔk]

38. Fruits. Nuts

fruit	frukt (m/f)	['frʉkt]
apple	eple (n)	['ɛplə]
pear	pære (m/f)	['pærə]
lemon	sitron (m)	[si'trʉn]
orange	appelsin (m)	[ɑpel'sin]
strawberry (garden ~)	jordbær (n)	['juːr‚bær]

tangerine	mandarin (m)	[mɑndɑ'rin]
plum	plomme (m/f)	['plʉmə]
peach	fersken (m)	['fæʂkən]
apricot	aprikos (m)	[ɑpri'kʉs]
raspberry	bringebær (n)	['briŋə‚bær]
pineapple	ananas (m)	['ɑnɑnɑs]

banana	banan (m)	[bɑ'nɑn]
watermelon	vannmelon (m)	['vɑnme‚lʉn]
grape	drue (m)	['drʉə]
sour cherry	kirsebær (n)	['çiʂə‚bær]
sweet cherry	morell (m)	[mʉ'rɛl]
melon	melon (m)	[me'lun]

grapefruit	grapefrukt (m/f)	['grɛjp‚frʉkt]
avocado	avokado (m)	[avɔ'kɑdɔ]
papaya	papaya (m)	[pɑ'paja]

mango	mango (m)	['maŋu]
pomegranate	granateple (n)	[gra'nɑt‚ɛplə]
redcurrant	rips (m)	['rips]
blackcurrant	solbær (n)	['sʊl‚bær]
gooseberry	stikkelsbær (n)	['stikəls‚bær]
bilberry	blåbær (n)	['blɔ‚bær]
blackberry	bjørnebær (m)	['bjœ:ŋə‚bær]
raisin	rosin (m)	[rʊ'sin]
fig	fiken (m)	['fikən]
date	daddel (m)	['dadəl]
peanut	jordnøtt (m)	['ju:r‚nœt]
almond	mandel (m)	['mandəl]
walnut	valnøtt (m/f)	['val‚nœt]
hazelnut	hasselnøtt (m/f)	['hasəl‚nœt]
coconut	kokosnøtt (m/f)	['kʊkʊs‚nœt]
pistachios	pistasier (m pl)	[pi'stɑsiər]

39. Bread. Sweets

bakers' confectionery (pastry)	bakevarer (m/f pl)	['bakə‚varər]
bread	brød (n)	['brø]
biscuits	kjeks (m)	['çɛks]
chocolate (n)	sjokolade (m)	[ʂʊkʊ'ladə]
chocolate (as adj)	sjokolade-	[ʂʊkʊ'ladə-]
candy (wrapped)	sukkertøy (n), karamell (m)	['sʉkə‚tøj], [kara'mɛl]
cake (e.g. cupcake)	kake (m/f)	['kakə]
cake (e.g. birthday ~)	bløtkake (m/f)	['bløt‚kakə]
pie (e.g. apple ~)	pai (m)	['paj]
filling (for cake, pie)	fyll (m/n)	['fʏl]
jam (whole fruit jam)	syltetøy (n)	['syltə‚tøj]
marmalade	marmelade (m)	[marme'ladə]
waffles	vaffel (m)	['vafəl]
ice-cream	iskrem (m)	['iskrɛm]
pudding (Christmas ~)	pudding (m)	['pʉdiŋ]

40. Cooked dishes

course, dish	rett (m)	['rɛt]
cuisine	kjøkken (n)	['çœkən]
recipe	oppskrift (m)	['ɔp‚skrift]
portion	porsjon (m)	[po'ʂʊn]
salad	salat (m)	[sa'lat]
soup	suppe (m/f)	['sʉpə]
clear soup (broth)	buljong (m)	[bu'ljoŋ]
sandwich (bread)	smørbrød (n)	['smør‚brø]

fried eggs	speilegg (n)	['spæjl,ɛg]
hamburger (beefburger)	hamburger (m)	['hamburgər]
beefsteak	biff (m)	['bif]

side dish	tilbehør (n)	['tilbə,hør]
spaghetti	spagetti (m)	[spɑ'gɛti]
mash	potetmos (m)	[pʊ'tet,mʊs]
pizza	pizza (m)	['pitsɑ]
porridge (oatmeal, etc.)	grøt (m)	['grøt]
omelette	omelett (m)	[ɔmə'let]

boiled (e.g. ~ beef)	kokt	['kʊkt]
smoked (adj)	røkt	['røkt]
fried (adj)	stekt	['stɛkt]
dried (adj)	tørket	['tœrkət]
frozen (adj)	frossen, dypfryst	['frɔsən], ['dyp,frʏst]
pickled (adj)	syltet	['sʏltət]

sweet (sugary)	søt	['søt]
salty (adj)	salt	['salt]
cold (adj)	kald	['kɑl]
hot (adj)	het, varm	['het], ['vɑrm]
bitter (adj)	bitter	['bitər]
tasty (adj)	lekker	['lekər]

to cook in boiling water	å koke	[ɔ 'kʊkə]
to cook (dinner)	å lage	[ɔ 'lɑgə]
to fry (vt)	å steke	[ɔ 'stekə]
to heat up (food)	å varme opp	[ɔ 'vɑrmə ɔp]

to salt (vt)	å salte	[ɔ 'sɑltə]
to pepper (vt)	å pepre	[ɔ 'pɛprə]
to grate (vt)	å rive	[ɔ 'rivə]
peel (n)	skall (n)	['skɑl]
to peel (vt)	å skrelle	[ɔ 'skrɛlə]

41. Spices

salt	salt (n)	['salt]
salty (adj)	salt	['salt]
to salt (vt)	å salte	[ɔ 'sɑltə]

black pepper	svart pepper (m)	['svɑːʈ 'pɛpər]
red pepper (milled ~)	rød pepper (m)	['rø 'pɛpər]
mustard	sennep (m)	['sɛnəp]
horseradish	pepperrot (m/f)	['pɛpər,rʊt]

condiment	krydder (n)	['krʏdər]
spice	krydder (n)	['krʏdər]
sauce	saus (m)	['saus]
vinegar	eddik (m)	['ɛdik]

anise	anis (m)	['ɑnis]
basil	basilik (m)	[bɑsi'lik]

cloves	nellik (m)	['nɛlik]
ginger	ingefær (m)	['iŋəˌfær]
coriander	koriander (m)	[kʊri'andər]
cinnamon	kanel (m)	[ka'nel]

sesame	sesam (m)	['sesam]
bay leaf	laurbærblad (n)	['laʊrbærˌbla]
paprika	paprika (m)	['paprika]
caraway	karve, kummin (m)	['karvə], ['kʉmin]
saffron	safran (m)	[sa'fran]

42. Meals

| food | mat (m) | ['mat] |
| to eat (vi, vt) | å spise | [ɔ 'spisə] |

breakfast	frokost (m)	['frʊkɔst]
to have breakfast	å spise frokost	[ɔ 'spisə ˌfrʊkɔst]
lunch	lunsj, lunch (m)	['lʉnʂ]
to have lunch	å spise lunsj	[ɔ 'spisə ˌlʉnʂ]
dinner	middag (m)	['miˌda]
to have dinner	å spise middag	[ɔ 'spisə 'miˌda]

| appetite | appetitt (m) | [ape'tit] |
| Enjoy your meal! | God appetitt! | ['gʊ ape'tit] |

to open (~ a bottle)	å åpne	[ɔ 'ɔpnə]
to spill (liquid)	å spille	[ɔ 'spilə]
to spill out (vi)	å bli spilt	[ɔ 'bli 'spilt]

to boil (vi)	å koke	[ɔ 'kʊkə]
to boil (vt)	å koke	[ɔ 'kʊkə]
boiled (~ water)	kokt	['kʊkt]

| to chill, cool down (vt) | å svalne | [ɔ 'svalnə] |
| to chill (vi) | å avkjøles | [ɔ 'avˌçœləs] |

| taste, flavour | smak (m) | ['smak] |
| aftertaste | bismak (m) | ['bismak] |

to slim down (lose weight)	å være på diet	[ɔ 'værə pɔ di'et]
diet	diett (m)	[di'et]
vitamin	vitamin (n)	[vita'min]
calorie	kalori (m)	[kalʊ'ri]

| vegetarian (n) | vegetarianer (m) | [vegetari'anər] |
| vegetarian (adj) | vegetarisk | [vege'tarisk] |

fats (nutrient)	fett (n)	['fɛt]
proteins	proteiner (n pl)	[prote'inər]
carbohydrates	kullhydrater (n pl)	['kʉlhyˌdratər]
slice (of lemon, ham)	skive (m/f)	['ʂivə]
piece (of cake, pie)	stykke (n)	['stʏkə]
crumb (of bread, cake, etc.)	smule (m)	['smʉlə]

43. Table setting

spoon	skje (m)	['ʂe]
knife	kniv (m)	['kniv]
fork	gaffel (m)	['gɑfəl]
cup (e.g., coffee ~)	kopp (m)	['kɔp]
plate (dinner ~)	tallerken (m)	[ta'lærkən]
saucer	tefat (n)	['te ̩fɑt]
serviette	serviett (m)	[sɛrvi'ɛt]
toothpick	tannpirker (m)	['tɑn ̩pirkər]

44. Restaurant

restaurant	restaurant (m)	[rɛstʊ'rɑŋ]
coffee bar	kafé, kaffebar (m)	[ka'fe], ['kɑfə ̩bɑr]
pub, bar	bar (m)	['bɑr]
tearoom	tesalong (m)	['tesɑ ̩lɔŋ]
waiter	servitør (m)	['særvi'tør]
waitress	servitrise (m/f)	[særvi'trisə]
barman	bartender (m)	['bɑː ̩tɛndər]
menu	meny (m)	[me'ny]
wine list	vinkart (n)	['vin ̩kɑːt]
to book a table	å reservere bord	[ɔ resɛr'verə 'bʊr]
course, dish	rett (m)	['rɛt]
to order (meal)	å bestille	[ɔ be'stilə]
to make an order	å bestille	[ɔ be'stilə]
aperitif	aperitiff (m)	[ɑperi'tif]
starter	forrett (m)	['fɔrɛt]
dessert, pudding	dessert (m)	[de'sɛːr]
bill	regning (m/f)	['rɛjniŋ]
to pay the bill	å betale regningen	[ɔ be'tɑlə 'rɛjniŋən]
to give change	å gi tilbake veksel	[ɔ ji til'bɑkə 'vɛksəl]
tip	driks (m)	['driks]

Family, relatives and friends

45. Personal information. Forms

name (first name)	**navn** (n)	['nɑvn]
surname (last name)	**etternavn** (n)	['ɛtə,nɑvn]
date of birth	**fødselsdato** (m)	['føtsəls,dɑtʊ]
place of birth	**fødested** (n)	['fødə,sted]
nationality	**nasjonalitet** (m)	[nɑʂʊnɑli'tet]
place of residence	**bosted** (n)	['bʊ,sted]
country	**land** (n)	['lɑn]
profession (occupation)	**yrke** (n), **profesjon** (m)	['yrkə], [prʊfe'ʂʊn]
gender, sex	**kjønn** (n)	['çœn]
height	**høyde** (m)	['højdə]
weight	**vekt** (m)	['vɛkt]

46. Family members. Relatives

mother	**mor** (m/f)	['mʊr]
father	**far** (m)	['fɑr]
son	**sønn** (m)	['sœn]
daughter	**datter** (m/f)	['dɑtər]
younger daughter	**yngste datter** (m/f)	['yŋstə 'dɑtər]
younger son	**yngste sønn** (m)	['yŋstə 'sœn]
eldest daughter	**eldste datter** (m/f)	['ɛlstə 'dɑtər]
eldest son	**eldste sønn** (m)	['ɛlstə 'sœn]
brother	**bror** (m)	['brʊr]
elder brother	**eldre bror** (m)	['ɛldrə ,brʊr]
younger brother	**lillebror** (m)	['lilə,brʊr]
sister	**søster** (m/f)	['søstər]
elder sister	**eldre søster** (m/f)	['ɛldrə ,søstər]
younger sister	**lillesøster** (m/f)	['lilə,søstər]
cousin (masc.)	**fetter** (m/f)	['fɛtər]
cousin (fem.)	**kusine** (m)	[kʊ'sinə]
mummy	**mamma** (m)	['mɑmɑ]
dad, daddy	**pappa** (m)	['pɑpɑ]
parents	**foreldre** (pl)	[for'ɛldrə]
child	**barn** (n)	['bɑːɳ]
children	**barn** (n pl)	['bɑːɳ]
grandmother	**bestemor** (m)	['bɛstə,mʊr]
grandfather	**bestefar** (m)	['bɛstə,fɑr]
grandson	**barnebarn** (n)	['bɑːɳə,bɑːɳ]

| granddaughter | barnebarn (n) | ['bɑːŋəˌbɑːŋ] |
| grandchildren | barnebarn (n pl) | ['bɑːŋəˌbɑːŋ] |

uncle	onkel (m)	['ʊnkəl]
aunt	tante (m/f)	['tɑntə]
nephew	nevø (m)	[ne'vø]
niece	niese (m/f)	[ni'esə]

mother-in-law (wife's mother)	svigermor (m/f)	['sviɡərˌmʊr]
father-in-law (husband's father)	svigerfar (m)	['sviɡərˌfɑr]
son-in-law (daughter's husband)	svigersønn (m)	['sviɡərˌsœn]
stepmother	stemor (m/f)	['steˌmʊr]
stepfather	stefar (m)	['steˌfɑr]

infant	brystbarn (n)	['brʏstˌbɑːŋ]
baby (infant)	spedbarn (n)	['speˌbɑːŋ]
little boy, kid	lite barn (n)	['litə 'bɑːŋ]

wife	kone (m/f)	['kʊnə]
husband	mann (m)	['mɑn]
spouse (husband)	ektemann (m)	['ɛktəˌmɑn]
spouse (wife)	hustru (m)	['hʊstrʉ]

married (masc.)	gift	['jift]
married (fem.)	gift	['jift]
single (unmarried)	ugift	[ʉ:'jift]
bachelor	ungkar (m)	['ʉŋˌkɑr]
divorced (masc.)	fraskilt	['frɑˌʂilt]
widow	enke (m)	['ɛnkə]
widower	enkemann (m)	['ɛnkəˌmɑn]

relative	slektning (m)	['ʂlektniŋ]
close relative	nær slektning (m)	['nær 'slektniŋ]
distant relative	fjern slektning (m)	['fjæːn 'slektniŋ]
relatives	slektninger (m pl)	['ʂlektniŋər]

orphan (boy or girl)	foreldreløst barn (n)	[for'ɛldrələst ˌbɑːŋ]
guardian (of a minor)	formynder (m)	['forˌmʏnər]
to adopt (a boy)	å adoptere	[ɔ adɔp'terə]
to adopt (a girl)	å adoptere	[ɔ adɔp'terə]

Medicine

47. Diseases

illness	sykdom (m)	['sʏkˌdɔm]
to be ill	å være syk	[ɔ 'værə 'syk]
health	helse (m/f)	['hɛlsə]

runny nose (coryza)	snue (m)	['snʉə]
tonsillitis	angina (m)	[an'gina]
cold (illness)	forkjølelse (m)	[fɔr'çœləlsə]
to catch a cold	å forkjøle seg	[ɔ fɔr'çœlə sæj]

bronchitis	bronkitt (m)	[brɔn'kit]
pneumonia	lungebetennelse (m)	['lʉŋə be'tɛnəlsə]
flu, influenza	influensa (m)	[inflʉ'ɛnsa]

shortsighted (adj)	nærsynt	['næˌsʏnt]
longsighted (adj)	langsynt	['laŋsʏnt]
strabismus (crossed eyes)	skjeløydhet (m)	['ʂɛløjdˌhet]
squint-eyed (adj)	skjeløyd	['ʂɛlˌøjd]
cataract	grå stær, katarakt (m)	['grɔ ˌstær], [kata'rakt]
glaucoma	glaukom (n)	[glaʉ'kɔm]

stroke	hjerneslag (n)	['jæːɳəˌslag]
heart attack	infarkt (n)	[in'farkt]
myocardial infarction	myokardieinfarkt (n)	['miɔ'kardiə in'farkt]
paralysis	paralyse, lammelse (m)	['para'lyse], ['lamǝlse]
to paralyse (vt)	å lamme	[ɔ 'lamə]

allergy	allergi (m)	[alæːˈgi]
asthma	astma (m)	['astma]
diabetes	diabetes (m)	[dia'betəs]

toothache	tannpine (m/f)	['tanˌpinə]
caries	karies (m)	['karies]

diarrhoea	diaré (m)	[dia'rɛ]
constipation	forstoppelse (m)	[fɔ'ʂtɔpəlsə]
stomach upset	magebesvær (m)	['magəˌbe'svær]
food poisoning	matforgiftning (m/f)	['matˌfɔr'jiftniŋ]
to get food poisoning	å få matforgiftning	[ɔ 'fɔ matˌfɔr'jiftniŋ]

arthritis	artritt (m)	[aːˈtrit]
rickets	rakitt (m)	[ra'kit]
rheumatism	revmatisme (m)	[revma'tismə]
atherosclerosis	arteriosklerose (m)	[aːˈteriʉskleˌrʉsə]

gastritis	magekatarr, gastritt (m)	['magəkaˌtar], [ˌga'strit]
appendicitis	appendisitt (m)	[apɛndi'sit]

cholecystitis	galleblærebetennelse (m)	['galə‚blærə be'tɛnəlsə]
ulcer	magesår (n)	['magə‚sɔr]

measles	meslinger (m pl)	['mɛs‚liŋər]
rubella (German measles)	røde hunder (m pl)	['rødə 'hʉnər]
jaundice	gulsott (m/f)	['gʉl‚sʊt]
hepatitis	hepatitt (m)	[hepa'tit]

schizophrenia	schizofreni (m)	[ʂisʉfre'ni]
rabies (hydrophobia)	rabies (m)	['rabiəs]
neurosis	nevrose (m)	[nev'rʉsə]
concussion	hjernerystelse (m)	['jæː‚nə‚rʏstəlsə]

cancer	kreft, cancer (m)	['krɛft], ['kansər]
sclerosis	sklerose (m)	[skle'rʉsə]
multiple sclerosis	multippel sklerose (m)	[mʉl'tipəl skle'rʉsə]

alcoholism	alkoholisme (m)	[alkʉhʊ'lismə]
alcoholic (n)	alkoholiker (m)	[alkʉ'hʊlikər]
syphilis	syfilis (m)	['syfilis]
AIDS	AIDS, aids (m)	['ɛjds]

tumour	svulst, tumor (m)	['svʉlst], [tʉ'mʊr]
malignant (adj)	ondartet, malign	['ʊn‚aːɭət], [ma'lign]
benign (adj)	godartet	['gʊ‚aːɭət]

fever	feber (m)	['febər]
malaria	malaria (m)	[ma'laria]
gangrene	koldbrann (m)	['kɔlbran]
seasickness	sjøsyke (m)	['ʂø‚sykə]
epilepsy	epilepsi (m)	[ɛpilep'si]

epidemic	epidemi (m)	[ɛpide'mi]
typhus	tyfus (m)	['tyfʉs]
tuberculosis	tuberkulose (m)	[tubærkʉ'lɔsə]
cholera	kolera (m)	['kʉlera]
plague (bubonic ~)	pest (m)	['pɛst]

48. Symptoms. Treatments. Part 1

symptom	symptom (n)	[sʏmp'tʊm]
temperature	temperatur (m)	[tɛmpəra'tʉr]
high temperature (fever)	høy temperatur (m)	['høj tɛmpəra'tʉr]
pulse	puls (m)	['pʉls]

dizziness (vertigo)	svimmelhet (m)	['sviməl‚het]
hot (adj)	varm	['vɑrm]
shivering	skjelving (m/f)	['ʂɛlviŋ]
pale (e.g. ~ face)	blek	['blek]

cough	hoste (m)	['hʊstə]
to cough (vi)	å hoste	[ɔ 'hʊstə]
to sneeze (vi)	å nyse	[ɔ 'nysə]
faint	besvimelse (m)	[bɛ'sviməlsə]

to faint (vi)	å besvime	[ɔ be'svimə]
bruise (hématome)	blåmerke (n)	['blɔˌmærkə]
bump (lump)	bule (m)	['bʉlə]
to bang (bump)	å slå seg	[ɔ 'slɔ sæj]
contusion (bruise)	blåmerke (n)	['blɔˌmærkə]
to get a bruise	å slå seg	[ɔ 'slɔ sæj]

to limp (vi)	å halte	[ɔ 'hɑltə]
dislocation	forvridning (m)	[fɔr'vridniŋ]
to dislocate (vt)	å forvri	[ɔ fɔr'vri]
fracture	brudd (n), fraktur (m)	['brʉd], [frɑk'tʉr]
to have a fracture	å få brudd	[ɔ 'fɔ 'brʉd]

cut (e.g. paper ~)	skjæresår (n)	['sæːrəˌsɔr]
to cut oneself	å skjære seg	[ɔ 'sæːrə sæj]
bleeding	blødning (m/f)	['blødniŋ]

burn (injury)	brannsår (n)	['brɑnˌsɔr]
to get burned	å brenne seg	[ɔ 'brɛnə sæj]

to prick (vt)	å stikke	[ɔ 'stikə]
to prick oneself	å stikke seg	[ɔ 'stikə sæj]
to injure (vt)	å skade	[ɔ 'skɑdə]
injury	skade (n)	['skɑdə]
wound	sår (n)	['sɔr]
trauma	traume (m)	['trɑʊmə]

to be delirious	å snakke i villelse	[ɔ 'snɑkə i 'viləlsə]
to stutter (vi)	å stamme	[ɔ 'stɑmə]
sunstroke	solstikk (n)	['sʉlˌstik]

49. Symptoms. Treatments. Part 2

pain, ache	smerte (m)	['smæːtə]
splinter (in foot, etc.)	flis (m/f)	['flis]

sweat (perspiration)	svette (m)	['svɛtə]
to sweat (perspire)	å svette	[ɔ 'svɛtə]
vomiting	oppkast (n)	['ɔpˌkɑst]
convulsions	kramper (m pl)	['krɑmpər]

pregnant (adj)	gravid	[grɑ'vid]
to be born	å fødes	[ɔ 'fødə]
delivery, labour	fødsel (m)	['føtsəl]
to deliver (~ a baby)	å føde	[ɔ 'fødə]
abortion	abort (m)	[ɑ'bɔːt]

breathing, respiration	åndedrett (n)	['ɔndəˌdrɛt]
in-breath (inhalation)	innånding (m/f)	['inˌɔniŋ]
out-breath (exhalation)	utånding (m/f)	['ʉtˌɔndiŋ]
to exhale (breathe out)	å puste ut	[ɔ 'pʉstə ʉt]
to inhale (vi)	å ånde inn	[ɔ 'ɔndə ˌin]
disabled person	handikappet person (m)	['hɑndiˌkɑpət pæ'ʂʉn]
cripple	krøpling (m)	['krøpliŋ]

49

drug addict	narkoman (m)	[narkʊ'man]
deaf (adj)	døv	['døv]
mute (adj)	stum	['stʉm]
deaf mute (adj)	døvstum	['døf͵stʉm]

mad, insane (adj)	gal	['gal]
madman (demented person)	gal mann (m)	['gal ͵man]
madwoman	gal kvinne (m/f)	['gal ͵kvinə]
to go insane	å bli sinnssyk	[ɔ 'bli 'sin͵syk]

gene	gen (m)	['gen]
immunity	immunitet (m)	[imʉni'tet]
hereditary (adj)	arvelig	['arvəli]
congenital (adj)	medfødt	['me:͵føt]

virus	virus (m)	['virʉs]
microbe	mikrobe (m)	[mi'krʊbə]
bacterium	bakterie (m)	[bak'teriə]
infection	infeksjon (m)	[infɛk'ʂʊn]

50. Symptoms. Treatments. Part 3

hospital	sykehus (n)	['sykə͵hʉs]
patient	pasient (m)	[pasi'ɛnt]

diagnosis	diagnose (m)	[dia'gnʊsə]
cure	kur (m)	['kʉr]
medical treatment	behandling (m/f)	[be'handliŋ]
to get treatment	å bli behandlet	[ɔ 'bli be'handlət]
to treat (~ a patient)	å behandle	[ɔ be'handlə]
to nurse (look after)	å skjøtte	[ɔ 'ʂøtə]
care (nursing ~)	sykepleie (m/f)	['sykə͵plæjə]

operation, surgery	operasjon (m)	[ɔpəra'ʂʊn]
to bandage (head, limb)	å forbinde	[ɔ for'binə]
bandaging	forbinding (m)	[for'biniŋ]

vaccination	vaksinering (m/f)	[vaksi'neriŋ]
to vaccinate (vt)	å vaksinere	[ɔ vaksi'nerə]
injection	injeksjon (m), sprøyte (m/f)	[injɛk'ʂʊn], ['sprøjtə]
to give an injection	å gi en sprøyte	[ɔ 'ji en 'sprøjtə]

attack	anfall (n)	['an͵fal]
amputation	amputasjon (m)	[ampʉta'ʂʊn]
to amputate (vt)	å amputere	[ɔ ampʉ'terə]
coma	koma (m)	['kʊma]
to be in a coma	å ligge i koma	[ɔ 'ligə i 'kʊma]
intensive care	intensivavdeling (m/f)	['inten͵siv 'av͵deliŋ]

to recover (~ from flu)	å bli frisk	[ɔ 'bli 'frisk]
condition (patient's ~)	tilstand (m)	['til͵stan]
consciousness	bevissthet (m)	[be'vist͵het]
memory (faculty)	minne (n), hukommelse (m)	['minə], [hʉ'kɔməlsə]

to pull out (tooth)	å trekke ut	[ɔ 'trɛkə ʉt]
filling	fylling (m/f)	['fʏliŋ]
to fill (a tooth)	å plombere	[ɔ plʉm'berə]

| hypnosis | hypnose (m) | [hʏp'nʉsə] |
| to hypnotize (vt) | å hypnotisere | [ɔ hʏpnʉti'serə] |

51. Doctors

doctor	lege (m)	['legə]
nurse	sykepleierske (m/f)	['sykə,plæjeʂkə]
personal doctor	personlig lege (m)	[pæ'ʂʉnli 'legə]

dentist	tannlege (m)	['tɑn,legə]
optician	øyelege (m)	['øjə,legə]
general practitioner	terapeut (m)	[terɑ'pɛut]
surgeon	kirurg (m)	[çi'rʉrg]

psychiatrist	psykiater (m)	[syki'ɑtər]
paediatrician	barnelege (m)	['bɑːŋə,legə]
psychologist	psykolog (m)	[sykʉ'lɔg]
gynaecologist	gynekolog (m)	[gynekʉ'lɔg]
cardiologist	kardiolog (m)	[kɑːdiʉ'lɔg]

52. Medicine. Drugs. Accessories

medicine, drug	medisin (m)	[medi'sin]
remedy	middel (n)	['midəl]
to prescribe (vt)	å ordinere	[ɔ ɔrdi'nerə]
prescription	resept (m)	[re'sɛpt]

tablet, pill	tablett (m)	[tɑb'let]
ointment	salve (m/f)	['sɑlvə]
ampoule	ampulle (m)	[ɑm'pʉlə]
mixture	mikstur (m)	[miks'tʉr]
syrup	sirup (m)	['sirʉp]
pill	pille (m/f)	['pilə]
powder	pulver (n)	['pʉlvər]

gauze bandage	gasbind (n)	['gɑs,bin]
cotton wool	vatt (m/n)	['vɑt]
iodine	jod (m/n)	['ʉd]

plaster	plaster (n)	['plɑstər]
eyedropper	pipette (m)	[pi'pɛtə]
thermometer	termometer (n)	[tɛrmʉ'metər]
syringe	sprøyte (m/f)	['sprøjtə]

wheelchair	rullestol (m)	['rʉlə,stʉl]
crutches	krykker (m/f pl)	['krʏkər]
painkiller	smertestillende middel (n)	['smæːtə,stilenə 'midəl]
laxative	laksativ (n)	[lɑksɑ'tiv]

spirits (ethanol)	sprit (m)	['sprit]
medicinal herbs	legeurter (m/f pl)	['legə,ʉːṭər]
herbal (~ tea)	urte-	['ʉːṭə-]

HUMAN HABITAT

City

53. City. Life in the city

city, town	**by** (m)	['by]
capital city	**hovedstad** (m)	['hʊvəd‚stad]
village	**landsby** (m)	['lans‚by]
city map	**bykart** (n)	['by‚kɑːt]
city centre	**sentrum** (n)	['sɛntrum]
suburb	**forstad** (m)	['fɔ‚stad]
suburban (adj)	**forstads-**	['fɔ‚stads-]
outskirts	**utkant** (m)	['ʉt‚kant]
environs (suburbs)	**omegner** (m pl)	['ɔm‚æjnər]
city block	**kvarter** (n)	[kvɑːʈer]
residential block (area)	**boligkvarter** (n)	['bʊli‚kvɑːʈer]
traffic	**trafikk** (m)	[trɑ'fik]
traffic lights	**trafikklys** (n)	[trɑ'fik‚lys]
public transport	**offentlig transport** (m)	['ɔfentli trans'pɔːt]
crossroads	**veikryss** (n)	['væjkrʏs]
zebra crossing	**fotgjengerovergang** (m)	['fʊt‚jɛŋər 'ɔvər‚gɑŋ]
pedestrian subway	**undergang** (m)	['ʉnər‚gɑŋ]
to cross (~ the street)	**å gå over**	[ɔ 'gɔ 'ɔvər]
pedestrian	**fotgjenger** (m)	['fʊt‚jɛŋər]
pavement	**fortau** (n)	['fɔː‚tɑʉ]
bridge	**bro** (m/f)	['brʊ]
embankment (river walk)	**kai** (m/f)	['kɑj]
fountain	**fontene** (m)	['fʊntnə]
allée (garden walkway)	**allé** (m)	[ɑ'leː]
park	**park** (m)	['pɑrk]
boulevard	**bulevard** (m)	[bule'vɑr]
square	**torg** (n)	['tɔr]
avenue (wide street)	**aveny** (m)	[ɑve'ny]
street	**gate** (m/f)	['gɑtə]
side street	**sidegate** (m/f)	['sidə‚gɑtə]
dead end	**blindgate** (m/f)	['blin‚gɑtə]
house	**hus** (n)	['hʉs]
building	**bygning** (m/f)	['bʏgniŋ]
skyscraper	**skyskraper** (m)	['ʂy‚skrɑpər]
facade	**fasade** (m)	[fɑ'sɑdə]
roof	**tak** (n)	['tɑk]

window	vindu (n)	['vindʉ]
arch	bue (m)	['bʉːə]
column	søyle (m)	['søjlə]
corner	hjørne (n)	['jœːnə]

shop window	utstillingsvindu (n)	['ʉtˌstiliŋs 'vindʉ]
signboard (store sign, etc.)	skilt (n)	['ʂilt]
poster	plakat (m)	[pla'kat]
advertising poster	reklameplakat (m)	[rɛ'klaməˌpla'kat]
hoarding	reklametavle (m/f)	[rɛ'klaməˌtavlə]

rubbish	søppel (m/f/n), avfall (n)	['sœpəl], ['avˌfal]
rubbish bin	søppelkasse (m/f)	['sœpəlˌkasə]
to litter (vi)	å kaste søppel	[ɔ 'kastə 'sœpəl]
rubbish dump	søppelfylling (m/f), deponi (n)	['sœpəlˌfʏliŋ], [ˌdepɔ'ni]

telephone box	telefonboks (m)	[tele'funˌbɔks]
lamppost	lyktestolpe (m)	['lʏktəˌstɔlpə]
bench (park ~)	benk (m)	['bɛŋk]

police officer	politi (m)	[pʊli'ti]
police	politi (n)	[pʊli'ti]
beggar	tigger (m)	['tigər]
homeless (n)	hjemløs	['jɛmˌløs]

54. Urban institutions

shop	forretning, butikk (m)	[fɔ'rɛtniŋ], [bʉ'tik]
chemist, pharmacy	apotek (n)	[apʉ'tek]
optician (spectacles shop)	optikk (m)	[ɔp'tik]
shopping centre	kjøpesenter (n)	['çøpəˌsɛntər]
supermarket	supermarked (n)	['sʉpəˌmarket]

bakery	bakeri (n)	[bake'ri]
baker	baker (m)	['bakər]
cake shop	konditori (n)	[kʊnditɔ'ri]
grocery shop	matbutikk (m)	['matbʉˌtik]
butcher shop	slakterbutikk (m)	['ʂlaktəbʉˌtik]

greengrocer	grønnsaksbutikk (m)	['grœnˌsaks bʉ'tik]
market	marked (n)	['markəd]

coffee bar	kafé, kaffebar (m)	[ka'fe], ['kafəˌbar]
restaurant	restaurant (m)	[rɛstʉ'raŋ]
pub, bar	pub (m)	['pʉb]
pizzeria	pizzeria (m)	[pitsə'ria]

hairdresser	frisørsalong (m)	[fri'sør saˌlɔŋ]
post office	post (m)	['pɔst]
dry cleaners	renseri (n)	[rɛnse'ri]
photo studio	fotostudio (n)	['fotoˌstʉdiɔ]

shoe shop	skobutikk (m)	['skʊˌbʉ'tik]
bookshop	bokhandel (m)	['bʊkˌhandəl]

sports shop	idrettsbutikk (m)	['idrɛts bʉ'tik]
clothes repair shop	reparasjon (m) av klær	[repɑrɑ'ʂʉn ɑ: ˌklær]
formal wear hire	leie (m/f) av klær	['læjə ɑ: ˌklær]
video rental shop	filmutleie (m/f)	['filmˌʉt'læje]

circus	sirkus (m/n)	['sirkʉs]
zoo	zoo, dyrepark (m)	['sʉ:], [dyrə'pɑrk]
cinema	kino (m)	['çinʉ]
museum	museum (n)	[mʉ'seum]
library	bibliotek (n)	[bibliʉ'tek]

theatre	teater (n)	[te'ɑtər]
opera (opera house)	opera (m)	['ʉperɑ]
nightclub	nattklubb (m)	['nɑtˌklʉb]
casino	kasino (n)	[kɑ'sinʉ]

mosque	moské (m)	[mʉ'ske]
synagogue	synagoge (m)	[synɑ'gʉgə]
cathedral	katedral (m)	[kate'drɑl]
temple	tempel (n)	['tɛmpəl]
church	kirke (m/f)	['çirkə]

college	institutt (n)	[insti'tʉt]
university	universitet (n)	[ʉnivæʂi'tet]
school	skole (m/f)	['skʉlə]

prefecture	prefektur (n)	[prɛfɛk'tʉr]
town hall	rådhus (n)	['rodˌhʉs]
hotel	hotell (n)	[hʉ'tɛl]
bank	bank (m)	['bɑnk]

embassy	ambassade (m)	[ɑmbɑ'sɑdə]
travel agency	reisebyrå (n)	['ræjsə byˌro]
information office	opplysningskontor (n)	[ɔp'lʏsniŋs kʉn'tʉr]
currency exchange	vekslingskontor (n)	['vɛkʂliŋs kʉn'tʉr]

| underground, tube | tunnelbane, T-bane (m) | ['tʉnəlˌbanə], ['tɛ:ˌbanə] |
| hospital | sykehus (n) | ['sykəˌhʉs] |

| petrol station | bensinstasjon (m) | [bɛn'sinˌstɑ'ʂʉn] |
| car park | parkeringsplass (m) | [pɑr'keriŋsˌplɑs] |

55. Signs

signboard (store sign, etc.)	skilt (n)	['ʂilt]
notice (door sign, etc.)	innskrift (m/f)	['inˌskrift]
poster	plakat, poster (m)	['plɑˌkɑt], ['pɔstər]
direction sign	veiviser (m)	['væjˌvisər]
arrow (sign)	pil (m/f)	['pil]

caution	advarsel (m)	['ɑdˌvaʂəl]
warning sign	varselskilt (n)	['vɑʂəlˌʂilt]
to warn (vt)	å varsle	[ɔ 'vɑʂlə]
rest day (weekly ~)	fridag (m)	['friˌdɑ]

timetable (schedule)	rutetabell (m)	['rʉtəˌtɑ'bɛl]
opening hours	åpningstider (m/f pl)	['ɔpniŋsˌtidər]
WELCOME!	VELKOMMEN!	['vɛlˌkɔmən]
ENTRANCE	INNGANG	['inˌgɑŋ]
WAY OUT	UTGANG	['ʉtˌgɑŋ]
PUSH	SKYV	['ʂyv]
PULL	TREKK	['trɛk]
OPEN	ÅPENT	['ɔpənt]
CLOSED	STENGT	['stɛŋt]
WOMEN	DAMER	['dɑmər]
MEN	HERRER	['hærər]
DISCOUNTS	RABATT	[rɑ'bɑt]
SALE	SALG	['sɑlg]
NEW!	NYTT!	['nʏt]
FREE	GRATIS	['grɑtis]
ATTENTION!	FORSIKTIG!	[fʉ'ʂiktə]
NO VACANCIES	INGEN LEDIGE ROM	['iŋən 'lediə rʉm]
RESERVED	RESERVERT	[resɛr'vɛ:t]
ADMINISTRATION	ADMINISTRASJON	[administrɑ'ʂʉn]
STAFF ONLY	KUN FOR ANSATTE	['kʉn fɔr ɑn'sɑtə]
BEWARE OF THE DOG!	VOKT DEM FOR HUNDEN	['vɔkt dem fɔ 'hʉnən]
NO SMOKING	RØYKING FORBUDT	['røjkiŋ fɔr'bʉt]
DO NOT TOUCH!	IKKE RØR!	['ikə 'rør]
DANGEROUS	FARLIG	['fɑ:ḻi]
DANGER	FARE	['fɑrə]
HIGH VOLTAGE	HØYSPENNING	['højˌspɛniŋ]
NO SWIMMING!	BADING FORBUDT	['bɑdiŋ fɔr'bʉt]
OUT OF ORDER	I USTAND	[i 'ʉˌstɑn]
FLAMMABLE	BRANNFARLIG	['brɑnˌfɑ:ḻi]
FORBIDDEN	FORBUDT	[fɔr'bʉt]
NO TRESPASSING!	INGEN INNKJØRING	['iŋən 'inˌçœriŋ]
WET PAINT	NYMALT	['nyˌmɑlt]

56. Urban transport

bus, coach	buss (m)	['bʉs]
tram	trikk (m)	['trik]
trolleybus	trolleybuss (m)	['trɔliˌbʉs]
route (of bus, etc.)	rute (m/f)	['rʉtə]
number (e.g. bus ~)	nummer (n)	['nʉmər]
to go by ...	å kjøre med ...	[ɔ 'çœ:rə me ...]
to get on (~ the bus)	å gå på ...	[ɔ 'gɔ pɔ ...]
to get off ...	å gå av ...	[ɔ 'gɔ ɑ: ...]
stop (e.g. bus ~)	holdeplass (m)	['hɔləˌplɑs]

next stop	neste holdeplass (m)	['nɛstə 'holə,plɑs]
terminus	endestasjon (m)	['ɛnə,stɑ'ʂʊn]
timetable	rutetabell (m)	['rʉtə,tɑ'bɛl]
to wait (vt)	å vente	[ɔ 'vɛntə]
ticket	billett (m)	[bi'let]
fare	billettpris (m)	[bi'let,pris]
cashier (ticket seller)	kasserer (m)	[kɑ'serər]
ticket inspection	billettkontroll (m)	[bi'let kʊn,trɔl]
ticket inspector	billett inspektør (m)	[bi'let inspɛk'tør]
to be late (for ...)	å komme for sent	[ɔ 'kɔmə fɔ'ʂɛnt]
to miss (~ the train, etc.)	å komme for sent til ...	[ɔ 'kɔmə fɔ'ʂɛnt til ...]
to be in a hurry	å skynde seg	[ɔ 'ʂynə sæj]
taxi, cab	drosje (m/f), taxi (m)	['drɔʂɛ], ['tɑksi]
taxi driver	taxisjåfør (m)	['tɑksi ʂɔ'før]
by taxi	med taxi	[me 'tɑksi]
taxi rank	taxiholdeplass (m)	['tɑksi 'hɔlə,plɑs]
to call a taxi	å taxi bestellen	[ɔ 'tɑksi be'stɛlən]
to take a taxi	å ta taxi	[ɔ 'tɑ ,tɑksi]
traffic	trafikk (m)	[trɑ'fik]
traffic jam	trafikkork (m)	[trɑ'fik,kɔrk]
rush hour	rushtid (m/f)	['rʉʂ,tid]
to park (vi)	å parkere	[ɔ pɑr'kerə]
to park (vt)	å parkere	[ɔ pɑr'kerə]
car park	parkeringsplass (m)	[pɑr'keriŋs,plɑs]
underground, tube	tunnelbane, T-bane (m)	['tʉnəl,bɑnə], ['tɛ:,bɑnə]
station	stasjon (m)	[stɑ'ʂʊn]
to take the tube	å kjøre med T-bane	[ɔ 'çœ:rə me 'tɛ:,bɑnə]
train	tog (n)	['tɔg]
train station	togstasjon (m)	['tɔg,stɑ'ʂʊn]

57. Sightseeing

monument	monument (n)	[mɔnʉ'mɛnt]
fortress	festning (m/f)	['fɛstniŋ]
palace	palass (n)	[pɑ'lɑs]
castle	borg (m)	['bɔrg]
tower	tårn (n)	['tɔ:n]
mausoleum	mausoleum (n)	[mausʊ'leum]
architecture	arkitektur (m)	[ɑrkitɛk'tʉr]
medieval (adj)	middelalderlig	['midəl,ɑldɛ:[i]
ancient (adj)	gammel	['gɑməl]
national (adj)	nasjonal	[nɑʂʊ'nɑl]
famous (monument, etc.)	kjent	['çɛnt]
tourist	turist (m)	[tʉ'rist]
guide (person)	guide (m)	['gɑjd]
excursion, sightseeing tour	utflukt (m/f)	['ʉt,flʉkt]

| to show (vt) | å vise | [ɔ 'visə] |
| to tell (vt) | å fortelle | [ɔ fɔ:'ʈɛlə] |

to find (vt)	å finne	[ɔ 'finə]
to get lost (lose one's way)	å gå seg bort	[ɔ 'gɔ sæj 'bu:t]
map (e.g. underground ~)	kart, linjekart (n)	['kɑ:t], ['linjə'kɑ:t]
map (e.g. city ~)	kart (n)	['kɑ:t]

souvenir, gift	suvenir (m)	[suve'nir]
gift shop	suvenirbutikk (m)	[suve'nir bu'tik]
to take pictures	å fotografere	[ɔ fɔtɔgrɑ'ferə]
to have one's picture taken	å bli fotografert	[ɔ 'bli fɔtɔgrɑ'fɛ:t]

58. Shopping

to buy (purchase)	å kjøpe	[ɔ 'çœ:pə]
shopping	innkjøp (n)	['in,çœp]
to go shopping	å gå shopping	[ɔ 'gɔ ,ʂɔpiŋ]
shopping	shopping (m)	['ʂɔpiŋ]

| to be open (ab. shop) | å være åpen | [ɔ 'værə 'ɔpən] |
| to be closed | å være stengt | [ɔ 'værə 'stɛŋt] |

footwear, shoes	skotøy (n)	['skutøj]
clothes, clothing	klær (n)	['klær]
cosmetics	kosmetikk (m)	[kusme'tik]
food products	matvarer (m/f pl)	['mɑt,vɑrər]
gift, present	gave (m/f)	['gɑvə]

| shop assistant (masc.) | forselger (m) | [fɔ'ʂɛlər] |
| shop assistant (fem.) | forselger (m) | [fɔ'ʂɛlər] |

cash desk	kasse (m/f)	['kɑsə]
mirror	speil (n)	['spæjl]
counter (shop ~)	disk (m)	['disk]
fitting room	prøverom (n)	['prøvə,rum]

to try on	å prøve	[ɔ 'prøvə]
to fit (ab. dress, etc.)	å passe	[ɔ 'pɑsə]
to fancy (vt)	å like	[ɔ 'likə]

price	pris (m)	['pris]
price tag	prislapp (m)	['pris,lɑp]
to cost (vt)	å koste	[ɔ 'kɔstə]
How much?	Hvor mye?	[vur 'mye]
discount	rabatt (m)	[rɑ'bɑt]

inexpensive (adj)	billig	['bili]
cheap (adj)	billig	['bili]
expensive (adj)	dyr	['dyr]
It's expensive	Det er dyrt	[de ær 'dy:t]

| hire (n) | utleie (m/f) | ['ʉt,læjə] |
| to hire (~ a dinner jacket) | å leie | [ɔ 'læjə] |

| credit (trade credit) | kreditt (m) | [krε'dit] |
| on credit (adv) | på kreditt | [pɔ krε'dit] |

59. Money

money	penger (m pl)	['pεŋər]
currency exchange	veksling (m/f)	['vεkşliŋ]
exchange rate	kurs (m)	['kuş]
cashpoint	minibank (m)	['mini‚bɑnk]
coin	mynt (m)	['mʏnt]

| dollar | dollar (m) | ['dɔlɑr] |
| euro | euro (m) | ['εʉrʉ] |

lira	lira (m)	['lire]
Deutschmark	mark (m/f)	['mɑrk]
franc	franc (m)	['frɑn]
pound sterling	pund sterling (m)	['pʉn stε:'liŋ]
yen	yen (m)	['jεn]

debt	skyld (m/f), gjeld (m)	['şyl], ['jεl]
debtor	skyldner (m)	['şylnər]
to lend (money)	å låne ut	[ɔ 'lo:nə ʉt]
to borrow (vi, vt)	å låne	[ɔ 'lo:nə]

bank	bank (m)	['bɑnk]
account	konto (m)	['kɔntʉ]
to deposit (vt)	å sette inn	[ɔ 'sεtə in]
to deposit into the account	å sette inn på kontoen	[ɔ 'sεtə in pɔ 'kɔntʉən]
to withdraw (vt)	å ta ut fra kontoen	[ɔ 'tɑ ʉt frɑ 'kɔntʉən]

credit card	kredittkort (n)	[krε'dit‚kɔ:t]
cash	kontanter (m pl)	[kʉn'tantər]
cheque	sjekk (m)	['şεk]
to write a cheque	å skrive en sjekk	[ɔ 'skrivə en 'şεk]
chequebook	sjekkbok (m/f)	['şεk‚bʉk]

wallet	lommebok (m)	['lʉmə‚bʉk]
purse	pung (m)	['pʉŋ]
safe	safe, seif (m)	['sεjf]

heir	arving (m)	['ɑrviŋ]
inheritance	arv (m)	['ɑrv]
fortune (wealth)	formue (m)	['for‚mʉə]

lease	leie (m)	['læjə]
rent (money)	husleie (m/f)	['hʉs‚læjə]
to rent (sth from sb)	å leie	[ɔ 'læjə]

price	pris (m)	['pris]
cost	kostnad (m)	['kɔstnɑd]
sum	sum (m)	['sʉm]
to spend (vt)	å bruke	[ɔ 'brʉkə]
expenses	utgifter (m/f pl)	['ʉt‚jiftər]

| to economize (vi, vt) | å spare | [ɔ 'spɑrə] |
| economical | sparsom | ['spɑʂɔm] |

to pay (vi, vt)	å betale	[ɔ be'tɑlə]
payment	betaling (m/f)	[be'tɑliŋ]
change (give the ~)	vekslepenger (pl)	['vɛkʂlə,pɛŋər]

tax	skatt (m)	['skɑt]
fine	bot (m/f)	['bʊt]
to fine (vt)	å bøtelegge	[ɔ 'bøtə,legə]

60. Post. Postal service

post office	post (m)	['pɔst]
post (letters, etc.)	post (m)	['pɔst]
postman	postbud (n)	['pɔst,bʉd]
opening hours	åpningstider (m/f pl)	['ɔpniŋs,tidər]

letter	brev (n)	['brev]
registered letter	rekommandert brev (n)	[rekʉmɑn'dɛ:ʈ ,brev]
postcard	postkort (n)	['pɔst,kɔ:ʈ]
telegram	telegram (n)	[tele'grɑm]
parcel	postpakke (m/f)	['pɔst,pɑkə]
money transfer	pengeoverføring (m/f)	['pɛŋə 'ɔvər,føriŋ]

to receive (vt)	å motta	[ɔ 'mɔtɑ]
to send (vt)	å sende	[ɔ 'sɛnə]
sending	avsending (m)	['ɑf,sɛniŋ]

address	adresse (m)	[ɑ'drɛsə]
postcode	postnummer (n)	['pɔst,nʉmər]
sender	avsender (m)	['ɑf,sɛnər]
receiver	mottaker (m)	['mɔt,tɑkər]

| name (first name) | fornavn (n) | ['fɔr,nɑvn] |
| surname (last name) | etternavn (n) | ['ɛtə,nɑvn] |

postage rate	tariff (m)	[tɑ'rif]
standard (adj)	vanlig	['vɑnli]
economical (adj)	økonomisk	[økʉ'nɔmisk]

weight	vekt (m)	['vɛkt]
to weigh (~ letters)	å veie	[ɔ 'væjə]
envelope	konvolutt (m)	[kʉnvʉ'lʉt]
postage stamp	frimerke (n)	['fri,mærkə]
to stamp an envelope	å sette på frimerke	[ɔ 'sɛtə pɔ 'fri,mærkə]

Dwelling. House. Home

61. House. Electricity

electricity	elektrisitet (m)	[εlektrisi'tet]
light bulb	lyspære (m/f)	['lys,pærə]
switch	strømbryter (m)	['strøm,brytər]
fuse (plug fuse)	sikring (m)	['sikriŋ]
cable, wire (electric ~)	ledning (m)	['ledniŋ]
wiring	ledningsnett (n)	['ledniŋs,nɛt]
electricity meter	elmåler (m)	['ɛl,molər]
readings	avlesninger (m/f pl)	['av,lesniŋər]

62. Villa. Mansion

country house	fritidshus (n)	['fritids,hʉs]
country-villa	villa (m)	['vila]
wing (~ of a building)	fløy (m)	['fløj]
garden	hage (m)	['hagə]
park	park (m)	['park]
tropical glasshouse	drivhus (n)	['driv,hʉs]
to look after (garden, etc.)	å ta vare	[ɔ 'ta ,varə]
swimming pool	svømmebasseng (n)	['svœmə,ba'sɛn]
gym (home gym)	gym (m)	['dʒym]
tennis court	tennisbane (m)	['tɛnis,banə]
home theater (room)	hjemmekino (m)	['jɛmə,çinʉ]
garage	garasje (m)	[ga'raṣə]
private property	privateiendom (m)	[pri'vat 'æjəndɔm]
private land	privat terreng (n)	[pri'vat tɛ'rɛŋ]
warning (caution)	advarsel (m)	['ad,vaṣəl]
warning sign	varselskilt (n)	['vaṣəl,ṣilt]
security	sikkerhet (m/f)	['sikər,het]
security guard	sikkerhetsvakt (m/f)	['sikərhɛts,vakt]
burglar alarm	tyverialarm (m)	[tyve'ri a'larm]

63. Flat

flat	leilighet (m/f)	['læjli,het]
room	rom (n)	['rʉm]
bedroom	soverom (n)	['sɔvə,rʉm]

dining room	spisestue (m/f)	['spisə‚stʉə]
living room	dagligstue (m/f)	['dagli‚stʉə]
study (home office)	arbeidsrom (n)	['arbæjds‚rʊm]

entry room	entré (m)	[an'trɛ:]
bathroom	bad, baderom (n)	['bad], ['badə‚rʊm]
water closet	toalett, WC (n)	[tʊa'let], [vɛ'sɛ]

ceiling	tak (n)	['tak]
floor	gulv (n)	['gʉlv]
corner	hjørne (n)	['jœ:ŋə]

64. Furniture. Interior

furniture	møbler (n pl)	['møblər]
table	bord (n)	['bʊr]
chair	stol (m)	['stʊl]
bed	seng (m/f)	['sɛŋ]

| sofa, settee | sofa (m) | ['sʊfa] |
| armchair | lenestol (m) | ['lenə‚stʊl] |

| bookcase | bokskap (n) | ['bʊk‚skap] |
| shelf | hylle (m/f) | ['hʏlə] |

wardrobe	klesskap (n)	['kle‚skap]
coat rack (wall-mounted ~)	knaggbrett (n)	['knag‚brɛt]
coat stand	stumtjener (m)	['stʉm‚tjenər]

| chest of drawers | kommode (m) | [kʊ'mʊdə] |
| coffee table | kaffebord (n) | ['kafə‚bʊr] |

mirror	speil (n)	['spæjl]
carpet	teppe (n)	['tɛpə]
small carpet	lite teppe (n)	['lite 'tɛpə]

fireplace	peis (m), ildsted (n)	['pæjs], ['ilsted]
candle	lys (n)	['lys]
candlestick	lysestake (m)	['lysə‚stakə]

drapes	gardiner (m/f pl)	[ga:'dinər]
wallpaper	tapet (n)	[ta'pet]
blinds (jalousie)	persienne (m)	[pæʂi'enə]

| table lamp | bordlampe (m/f) | ['bʊr‚lampə] |
| wall lamp (sconce) | vegglampe (m/f) | ['vɛg‚lampə] |

| standard lamp | gulvlampe (m/f) | ['gʉlv‚lampə] |
| chandelier | lysekrone (m/f) | ['lysə‚krʊnə] |

leg (of chair, table)	bein (n)	['bæjn]
armrest	armlene (n)	['arm‚lenə]
back (backrest)	rygg (m)	['rʏg]
drawer	skuff (m)	['skʉf]

65. Bedding

bedclothes	sengetøy (n)	['sɛŋə,tøj]
pillow	pute (m/f)	['pʉtə]
pillowslip	putevar, putetrekk (n)	['pʉtə,var], ['pʉtə,trɛk]
duvet	dyne (m/f)	['dynə]
sheet	laken (n)	['lakən]
bedspread	sengeteppe (n)	['sɛŋə,tɛpə]

66. Kitchen

kitchen	kjøkken (n)	['çœkən]
gas	gass (m)	['gɑs]
gas cooker	gasskomfyr (m)	['gɑs kɔm,fyr]
electric cooker	elektrisk komfyr (m)	[ɛ'lektrisk kɔm,fyr]
oven	bakeovn (m)	['bakə,ɔvn]
microwave oven	mikrobølgeovn (m)	['mikrʉ,bølgə'ɔvn]

refrigerator	kjøleskap (n)	['çœlə,skap]
freezer	fryser (m)	['frysər]
dishwasher	oppvaskmaskin (m)	['ɔpvask ma,ʂin]

mincer	kjøttkvern (m/f)	['çœt,kvɛ:ɳ]
juicer	juicepresse (m/f)	['dʒʉs,prɛsə]
toaster	brødrister (m)	['brø,ristər]
mixer	mikser (m)	['miksər]

coffee machine	kaffetrakter (m)	['kafə,traktər]
coffee pot	kaffekanne (m/f)	['kafə,kanə]
coffee grinder	kaffekvern (m/f)	['kafə,kvɛ:ɳ]

kettle	tekjele (m)	['te,çelə]
teapot	tekanne (m/f)	['te,kanə]
lid	lokk (n)	['lɔk]
tea strainer	tesil (m)	['te,sil]

spoon	skje (m)	['ʂe]
teaspoon	teskje (m)	['te,ʂe]
soup spoon	spiseskje (m)	['spisə,ʂɛ]
fork	gaffel (m)	['gafəl]
knife	kniv (m)	['kniv]

tableware (dishes)	servise (n)	[sær'visə]
plate (dinner ~)	tallerken (m)	[ta'lærkən]
saucer	tefat (n)	['te,fat]

shot glass	shotglass (n)	['ʂɔt,glɑs]
glass (tumbler)	glass (n)	['glɑs]
cup	kopp (m)	['kɔp]

sugar bowl	sukkerskål (m/f)	['sʉkər,skɔl]
salt cellar	saltbøsse (m/f)	['salt,bøsə]
pepper pot	pepperbøsse (m/f)	['pɛpər,bøsə]

butter dish	smørkopp (m)	['smœr,kɔp]
stock pot (soup pot)	gryte (m/f)	['grytə]
frying pan (skillet)	steikepanne (m/f)	['stæjkə,panə]
ladle	sleiv (m/f)	['ʂlæjv]
colander	dørslag (n)	['dœʂlag]
tray (serving ~)	brett (n)	['brɛt]

bottle	flaske (m)	['flaskə]
jar (glass)	glasskrukke (m/f)	['glas,krʉkə]
tin (can)	boks (m)	['bɔks]

bottle opener	flaskeåpner (m)	['flaskə,ɔpnər]
tin opener	konservåpner (m)	['kʉnsəv,ɔpnər]
corkscrew	korketrekker (m)	['kɔrkə,trɛkər]
filter	filter (n)	['filtər]
to filter (vt)	å filtrere	[ɔ fil'trerə]

| waste (food ~, etc.) | søppel (m/f/n) | ['sœpəl] |
| waste bin (kitchen ~) | søppelbøtte (m/f) | ['sœpəl,bœtə] |

67. Bathroom

bathroom	bad, baderom (n)	['bad], ['badə,rʉm]
water	vann (n)	['van]
tap	kran (m/f)	['kran]
hot water	varmt vann (n)	['varmt ,van]
cold water	kaldt vann (n)	['kalt van]

toothpaste	tannpasta (m)	['tan,pasta]
to clean one's teeth	å pusse tennene	[ɔ 'pʉsə 'tɛnənə]
toothbrush	tannbørste (m)	['tan,bœʂtə]

to shave (vi)	å barbere seg	[ɔ bar'berə sæj]
shaving foam	barberskum (n)	[bar'bɛ,skʉm]
razor	høvel (m)	['høvəl]

to wash (one's hands, etc.)	å vaske	[ɔ 'vaskə]
to have a bath	å vaske seg	[ɔ 'vaskə sæj]
shower	dusj (m)	['dʉʂ]
to have a shower	å ta en dusj	[ɔ 'ta en 'dʉʂ]

bath	badekar (n)	['badə,kar]
toilet (toilet bowl)	toalettstol (m)	[tʉa'let,stʉl]
sink (washbasin)	vaskeservant (m)	['vaskə,sɛr'vant]

| soap | såpe (m/f) | ['so:pə] |
| soap dish | såpeskål (m/f) | ['so:pə,skɔl] |

sponge	svamp (m)	['svamp]
shampoo	sjampo (m)	['ʂam,pʉ]
towel	håndkle (n)	['hɔn,klɛ]
bathrobe	badekåpe (m/f)	['badə,ko:pə]
laundry (process)	vask (m)	['vask]
washing machine	vaskemaskin (m)	['vaskə ma,ʂin]

| to do the laundry | å vaske tøy | [ɔ 'vaskə 'tøj] |
| washing powder | vaskepulver (n) | ['vaskə,pʉlvər] |

68. Household appliances

TV, telly	TV (m), TV-apparat (n)	['tɛvɛ], ['tɛvɛ apa'rat]
tape recorder	båndopptaker (m)	['bɔn,ɔptakər]
video	video (m)	['videʉ]
radio	radio (m)	['radiʉ]
player (CD, MP3, etc.)	spiller (m)	['spilər]

video projector	videoprojektor (m)	['videʉ prɔ'jɛktɔr]
home cinema	hjemmekino (m)	['jɛmə,çinʉ]
DVD player	DVD-spiller (m)	[deve'de ,spilər]
amplifier	forsterker (m)	[fɔ'ʂtærkər]
video game console	spillkonsoll (m)	['spil kʉn'sɔl]

video camera	videokamera (n)	['videʉ ,kamera]
camera (photo)	kamera (n)	['kamera]
digital camera	digitalkamera (n)	[digi'tal ,kamera]

vacuum cleaner	støvsuger (m)	['støf,sʉgər]
iron (e.g. steam ~)	strykejern (n)	['strykə,jæː,n]
ironing board	strykebrett (n)	['strykə,brɛt]

telephone	telefon (m)	[tele'fʉn]
mobile phone	mobiltelefon (m)	[mʉ'bil tele'fʉn]
typewriter	skrivemaskin (m)	['skrivə ma,ʂin]
sewing machine	symaskin (m)	['siːma,ʂin]

microphone	mikrofon (m)	[mikrʉ'fʉn]
headphones	hodetelefoner (n pl)	['hɔdetelə,fʉnər]
remote control (TV)	fjernkontroll (m)	['fjæː,ŋ kʉn'trɔl]

CD, compact disc	CD-rom (m)	['sɛdɛ,rʉm]
cassette, tape	kassett (m)	[ka'sɛt]
vinyl record	plate, skive (m/f)	['platə], ['ʂivə]

Job. Business. Part 1

69. Office. Working in the office

office (company ~)	kontor (n)	[kʊn'tʊr]
office (of director, etc.)	kontor (n)	[kʊn'tʊr]
reception desk	resepsjon (m)	[resɛp'ʂʊn]
secretary	sekretær (m)	[sɛkrə'tær]
secretary (fem.)	sekretær (m)	[sɛkrə'tær]
director	direktør (m)	[dirɛk'tør]
manager	manager (m)	['mɛnidʒər]
accountant	regnskapsfører (m)	['rɛjnskaps̩førər]
employee	ansatt (n)	['an̩sat]
furniture	møbler (n pl)	['møblər]
desk	bord (n)	['bʊr]
desk chair	arbeidsstol (m)	['arbæjds̩stʊl]
drawer unit	skuffeseksjon (m)	['skʉfə̩sɛk'ʂʊn]
coat stand	stumtjener (m)	['stʉm̩tjenər]
computer	datamaskin (m)	['data ma̩ʂin]
printer	skriver (m)	['skrivər]
fax machine	faks (m)	['faks]
photocopier	kopimaskin (m)	[kʊ'pi ma̩ʂin]
paper	papir (n)	[pa'pir]
office supplies	kontorartikler (m pl)	[kʊn'tʊr aː'ţiklər]
mouse mat	musematte (m/f)	['mʉsə̩matə]
sheet of paper	ark (n)	['ark]
binder	mappe (m/f)	['mapə]
catalogue	katalog (m)	[kata'log]
phone directory	telefonkatalog (m)	[tele'fʊn kata'log]
documentation	dokumentasjon (m)	[dokʉmɛnta'ʂʊn]
brochure (e.g. 12 pages ~)	brosjyre (m)	[bro'ʂyrə]
leaflet (promotional ~)	reklameblad (n)	[rɛ'klamə̩bla]
sample	prøve (m)	['prøvə]
training meeting	trening (m/f)	['treniŋ]
meeting (of managers)	møte (n)	['møtə]
lunch time	lunsj pause (m)	['lʉnʂ ̩paʊsə]
to make a copy	å lage en kopi	[ɔ 'lagə en kʊ'pi]
to make multiple copies	å kopiere	[ɔ kʊ'pjerə]
to receive a fax	å motta faks	[ɔ 'mota ̩faks]
to send a fax	å sende faks	[ɔ 'sɛnə ̩faks]
to call (by phone)	å ringe	[ɔ 'riŋə]
to answer (vt)	å svare	[ɔ 'svarə]

to put through	å sætte over til ...	[ɔ 'sætə 'ɔvər til ...]
to arrange, to set up	å arrangere	[ɔ arɑŋ'ʂerə]
to demonstrate (vt)	å demonstrere	[ɔ demɔn'strerə]
to be absent	å være fraværende	[ɔ 'værə 'frɑˌværənə]
absence	fravær (n)	['frɑˌvær]

70. Business processes. Part 1

business	bedrift, handel (m)	[be'drift], ['hɑndəl]
occupation	yrke (n)	['yrkə]
firm	firma (n)	['firmɑ]
company	foretak (n)	['forəˌtak]
corporation	korporasjon (m)	[kʊrpʊrɑ'ʂʊn]
enterprise	foretak (n)	['forəˌtak]
agency	agentur (n)	[agɛn'tʉr]

agreement (contract)	avtale (m)	['avˌtalə]
contract	kontrakt (m)	[kʊn'trakt]
deal	avtale (m)	['avˌtalə]
order (to place an ~)	bestilling (m)	[be'stiliŋ]
terms (of the contract)	vilkår (n)	['vilˌkɔːr]

wholesale (adv)	en gros	[ɛn 'grɔ]
wholesale (adj)	engros-	[ɛŋ'grɔ-]
wholesale (n)	engroshandel (m)	[ɛŋ'grɔˌhɑndəl]
retail (adj)	detalj-	[de'talj-]
retail (n)	detaljhandel (m)	[de'taljˌhɑndəl]

competitor	konkurrent (m)	[kʊnkʉ'rɛnt]
competition	konkurranse (m)	[kʊnkʉ'rɑnsə]
to compete (vi)	å konkurrere	[ɔ kʊnkʉ'rerə]

| partner (associate) | partner (m) | ['pɑːʈnər] |
| partnership | partnerskap (n) | ['pɑːʈnəˌskɑp] |

crisis	krise (m/f)	['krisə]
bankruptcy	fallitt (m)	[fɑ'lit]
to go bankrupt	å gå konkurs	[ɔ 'gɔ kɔn'kʉʂ]
difficulty	vanskelighet (m)	['vanskəliˌhet]
problem	problem (n)	[prʊ'blem]
catastrophe	katastrofe (m)	[kɑtɑ'strɔfə]

economy	økonomi (m)	[økʊnʊ'mi]
economic (~ growth)	økonomisk	[økʉ'nɔmisk]
economic recession	økonomisk nedgang (m)	[økʉ'nɔmisk 'nedˌgɑŋ]

| goal (aim) | mål (n) | ['mɔl] |
| task | oppgave (m/f) | ['ɔpˌgɑvə] |

to trade (vi)	å handle	[ɔ 'hɑndlə]
network (distribution ~)	nettverk (n)	['nɛtˌværk]
inventory (stock)	lager (n)	['lɑgər]
range (assortment)	sortiment (n)	[sɔːʈi'mɛn]
leader (leading company)	leder (m)	['ledər]

| large (~ company) | stor | ['stʊr] |
| monopoly | monopol (n) | [mʊnʊ'pɔl] |

theory	teori (m)	[teʊ'ri]
practice	praksis (m)	['praksis]
experience (in my ~)	erfaring (m/f)	[ær'fariŋ]
trend (tendency)	tendens (m)	[tɛn'dɛns]
development	utvikling (m/f)	['ʉt,viklin]

71. Business processes. Part 2

| profit (foregone ~) | utbytte (n), fordel (m) | ['ʉt,bʏtə], ['fɔ:d̪el] |
| profitable (~ deal) | fordelaktig | [fɔ:d̪el'akti] |

delegation (group)	delegasjon (m)	[delega'ʂʊn]
salary	lønn (m/f)	['lœn]
to correct (an error)	å rette	[ɔ 'rɛtə]
business trip	forretningsreise (m/f)	[fɔ'rɛtniŋs,ræjsə]
commission	provisjon (m)	[prʊvi'ʂʊn]

to control (vt)	å kontrollere	[ɔ kʊntrɔ'lerə]
conference	konferanse (m)	[kʊnfə'ransə]
licence	lisens (m)	[li'sɛns]
reliable (~ partner)	pålitelig	[pɔ'liteli]

initiative (undertaking)	initiativ (n)	[initsia'tiv]
norm (standard)	norm (m)	['nɔrm]
circumstance	omstendighet (m)	[ɔm'stɛndi,het]
duty (of employee)	plikt (m/f)	['plikt]

organization (company)	organisasjon (m)	[ɔrganisa'ʂʊn]
organization (process)	organisering (m)	[ɔrgani'seriŋ]
organized (adj)	organisert	[ɔrgani'sɛ:t]
cancellation	avlysning (m/f)	['av,lʏsniŋ]
to cancel (call off)	å avlyse, å annullere	[ɔ 'av,lysə], [ɔ anʉ'lerə]
report (official ~)	rapport (m)	[ra'pɔ:t]

patent	patent (n)	[pa'tɛnt]
to patent (obtain patent)	å patentere	[ɔ paten'terə]
to plan (vt)	å planlegge	[ɔ 'plan,legə]

bonus (money)	gratiale (n)	[gratsi'a:lə]
professional (adj)	professionel	[prʊ'fɛsiɔ,nɛl]
procedure	prosedyre (m)	[prʊsə'dyrə]

to examine (contract, etc.)	å undersøke	[ɔ 'ʉnə,søkə]
calculation	beregning (m/f)	[be'rɛjniŋ]
reputation	rykte (n)	['rʏktə]
risk	risiko (m)	['risikʊ]

to manage, to run	å styre, å lede	[ɔ 'styrə], [ɔ 'ledə]
information	opplysninger (m/f pl)	['ɔp,lʏsniŋər]
property	eiendom (m)	['æjən,dɔm]
union	forbund (n)	['fɔr,bʉn]

life insurance	livsforsikring (m/f)	['lifsfɔ‚sikriŋ]
to insure (vt)	å forsikre	[ɔ fɔ'sikrə]
insurance	forsikring (m/f)	[fɔ'sikriŋ]

auction (~ sale)	auksjon (m)	[aʊk'ʂʊn]
to notify (inform)	å underrette	[ɔ 'ʉnə‚rɛtə]
management (process)	ledelse (m)	['ledəlsə]
service (~ industry)	tjeneste (m)	['tjenɛstə]

forum	forum (n)	['fɔrum]
to function (vi)	å fungere	[ɔ fʉ'ŋerə]
stage (phase)	etappe (m)	[e'tapə]
legal (~ services)	juridisk	[jʉ'ridisk]
lawyer (legal advisor)	jurist (m)	[jʉ'rist]

72. Production. Works

plant	verk (n)	['værk]
factory	fabrikk (m)	[fɑ'brik]
workshop	verkstad (m)	['værk‚stad]
works, production site	produksjonsplass (m)	[prʊdʊk'ʂʊns ‚plas]

industry (manufacturing)	industri (m)	[indʉ'stri]
industrial (adj)	industriell	[indʉstri'ɛl]
heavy industry	tungindustri (m)	['tʉŋ ‚indʉ'stri]
light industry	lettindustri (m)	['let‚indʉ'stri]

products	produksjon (m)	[prʊdʉk'ʂʊn]
to produce (vt)	å produsere	[ɔ prʊdʉ'serə]
raw materials	råstoffer (n pl)	['rɔ‚stɔfər]

foreman (construction ~)	formann, bas (m)	['fɔrman], ['bas]
workers team (crew)	arbeidslag (n)	['arbæjds‚lag]
worker	arbeider (m)	['ar‚bæjdər]

working day	arbeidsdag (m)	['arbæjds‚da]
pause (rest break)	hvilepause (m)	['vilə‚paʊse]
meeting	møte (n)	['møtə]
to discuss (vt)	å drøfte, å diskutere	[ɔ 'drœftə], [ɔ diskʉ'terə]

plan	plan (m)	['plan]
to fulfil the plan	å oppfylle planen	[ɔ 'ɔp‚fʏlə 'planən]
rate of output	produksjonsmål (n)	[prʊdʊk'ʂʊns ‚mol]
quality	kvalitet (m)	[kvali'tɛt]
control (checking)	kontroll (m)	[kʊn'trɔl]
quality control	kvalitetskontroll (m)	[kvali'tɛt kʊn'trɔl]

workplace safety	arbeidervern (n)	['arbæjdər‚væ:n]
discipline	disiplin (m)	[disip'lin]
violation (of safety rules, etc.)	brudd (n)	['brʉd]
to violate (rules)	å bryte	[ɔ 'brytə]

| strike | streik (m) | ['stræjk] |
| striker | streiker (m) | ['stræjkər] |

to be on strike	å streike	[ɔ 'stræjkə]
trade union	fagforening (m/f)	['fɑgfɔˌreniŋ]

to invent (machine, etc.)	å oppfinne	[ɔ 'ɔpˌfinə]
invention	oppfinnelse (m)	['ɔpˌfinəlsə]
research	forskning (m)	['fɔːʂkniŋ]
to improve (make better)	å forbedre	[ɔ fɔr'bɛdrə]
technology	teknologi (m)	[tɛknʊlʊ'gi]
technical drawing	teknisk tegning (m/f)	['tɛknisk ˌtæjniŋ]

load, cargo	last (m/f)	['lɑst]
loader (person)	lastearbeider (m)	['lɑstə'arˌbæjdər]
to load (vehicle, etc.)	å laste	[ɔ 'lɑstə]
loading (process)	lasting (m/f)	['lɑstiŋ]
to unload (vi, vt)	å lesse av	[ɔ 'lese ɑː]
unloading	avlessing (m/f)	['ɑvˌlesiŋ]

transport	transport (m)	[trɑns'pɔːt]
transport company	transportfirma (n)	[trɑns'pɔːt ˌfirmɑ]
to transport (vt)	å transportere	[ɔ trɑnspɔːˈʈerə]

wagon	godsvogn (m/f)	['gʊtsˌvɔŋn]
tank (e.g., oil ~)	tank (m)	['tɑnk]
lorry	lastebil (m)	['lɑstəˌbil]

machine tool	verktøymaskin (m)	['værktøj maˌʂin]
mechanism	mekanisme (m)	[mekɑ'nismə]

industrial waste	industrielt avfall (n)	[indʉstri'ɛlt 'ɑvˌfɑl]
packing (process)	pakning (m/f)	['pɑkniŋ]
to pack (vt)	å pakke	[ɔ 'pɑkə]

73. Contract. Agreement

contract	kontrakt (m)	[kʊn'trɑkt]
agreement	avtale (m)	['ɑvˌtɑlə]
addendum	tillegg, bilag (n)	['tiˌleg], ['biˌlɑg]

to sign a contract	å inngå kontrakt	[ɔ 'inˌgɔ kʊn'trɑkt]
signature	underskrift (m/f)	['ʉnəˌskrift]
to sign (vt)	å underskrive	[ɔ 'ʉnəˌskrivə]
seal (stamp)	stempel (n)	['stɛmpəl]

subject of contract	kontraktens gjenstand (m)	[kʊn'trɑktəns 'jɛnˌstɑn]
clause	klausul (m)	[klɑʊ'sʉl]
parties (in contract)	parter (m pl)	['pɑːtər]
legal address	juridisk adresse (m/f)	[jʉ'ridisk ɑ'drɛsə]

to violate the contract	å bryte kontrakten	[ɔ 'brytə kʊn'trɑktən]
commitment (obligation)	forpliktelse (m)	[fɔr'pliktəlsə]
responsibility	ansvar (n)	['ɑnˌsvɑr]
force majeure	force majeure (m)	[ˌfɔrs mɑ'ʒøːr]
dispute	tvist (m)	['tvist]
penalties	straffeavgifter (m pl)	['strɑfə ɑv'jiftər]

74. Import & Export

import	**import** (m)	[im'pɔːt]
importer	**importør** (m)	[impɔː'tør]
to import (vt)	**å importere**	[ɔ impɔː'terə]
import (as adj.)	**import-**	[im'pɔːt-]
export (exportation)	**eksport** (m)	[ɛks'pɔːt]
exporter	**eksportør** (m)	[ɛkspɔː'tør]
to export (vi, vt)	**å eksportere**	[ɔ ɛkspɔː'terə]
export (as adj.)	**eksport-**	[ɛks'pɔːt-]
goods (merchandise)	**vare** (m/f)	['varə]
consignment, lot	**parti** (n)	[pɑː'ʧi]
weight	**vekt** (m)	['vɛkt]
volume	**volum** (n)	[vɔ'lʉm]
cubic metre	**kubikkmeter** (m)	[kʉ'bik‚metər]
manufacturer	**produsent** (m)	[prʉdʉ'sɛnt]
transport company	**transportfirma** (n)	[trans'pɔːt ‚firmɑ]
container	**container** (m)	[kɔn'tɛjnər]
border	**grense** (m/f)	['grɛnsə]
customs	**toll** (m)	['tɔl]
customs duty	**tollavgift** (m)	['tɔl ɑv'jift]
customs officer	**tollbetjent** (m)	['tɔlbe‚tjɛnt]
smuggling	**smugling** (m/f)	['smʉgliŋ]
contraband (smuggled goods)	**smuglergods** (n)	['smʉglə‚gʉts]

75. Finances

share, stock	**aksje** (m)	['ɑkʂə]
bond (certificate)	**obligasjon** (m)	[ɔbligɑ'ʂʉn]
promissory note	**veksel** (m)	['vɛksəl]
stock exchange	**børs** (m)	['bœʂ]
stock price	**aksjekurs** (m)	['ɑkʂə‚kʉʂ]
to go down (become cheaper)	**å gå ned**	[ɔ 'gɔ ne]
to go up (become more expensive)	**å gå opp**	[ɔ 'gɔ ɔp]
share	**andel** (m)	['ɑn‚del]
controlling interest	**aksjemajoritet** (m)	['ɑkʂə‚mɑjɔri'tet]
investment	**investering** (m/f)	[inve'steriŋ]
to invest (vt)	**å investere**	[ɔ inve'sterə]
percent	**prosent** (m)	[prʉ'sɛnt]
interest (on investment)	**rente** (m/f)	['rɛntə]
profit	**profitt** (m), **fortjeneste** (m/f)	[prɔ'fit], [fɔː'tjenɛstə]
profitable (adj)	**profitabel**	[prɔfi'tabəl]

tax	skatt (m)	['skɑt]
currency (foreign ~)	valuta (m)	[vɑ'lʉtɑ]
national (adj)	nasjonal	[nɑʂʉ'nɑl]
exchange (currency ~)	veksling (m/f)	['vɛkʂliŋ]

| accountant | regnskapsfører (m) | ['rɛjnskɑps,førər] |
| accounting | bokføring (m/f) | ['bʊk'føriŋ] |

bankruptcy	fallitt (m)	[fɑ'lit]
collapse, ruin	krakk (n)	['krɑk]
ruin	ruin (m)	[rʉ'in]
to be ruined (financially)	å ruinere seg	[ɔ rʉi'nerə sæj]
inflation	inflasjon (m)	[inflɑ'ʂʊn]
devaluation	devaluering (m)	[devɑlʉ'eriŋ]

capital	kapital (m)	[kɑpi'tɑl]
income	inntekt (m/f), innkomst (m)	['in,tɛkt], ['in,kɔmst]
turnover	omsetning (m/f)	['ɔm,sɛtniŋ]
resources	ressurser (m pl)	[re'sʉʂər]
monetary resources	pengemidler (m pl)	['pɛŋə,midlər]
overheads	faste utgifter (m/f pl)	['fɑstə 'ʉt,jiftər]
to reduce (expenses)	å redusere	[ɔ redʉ'serə]

76. Marketing

marketing	markedsføring (m/f)	['mɑrkəds,føriŋ]
market	marked (n)	['mɑrkəd]
market segment	markedssegment (n)	['mɑrkəds seg'mɛnt]
product	produkt (n)	[prʉ'dʉkt]
goods (merchandise)	vare (m/f)	['vɑrə]
brand	merkenavn (n)	['mærkə,nɑvn]
trademark	varemerke (n)	['vɑrə,mærkə]
logotype	firmamerke (n)	['firmɑ,mærkə]
logo	logo (m)	['lugʉ]

demand	etterspørsel (m)	['ɛtə,spœəʂəl]
supply	tilbud (n)	['til,bʉd]
need	behov (n)	[be'hʊv]
consumer	forbruker (m)	[for'brʉkər]
analysis	analyse (m)	[ɑnɑ'lysə]
to analyse (vt)	å analysere	[ɔ ɑnɑly'serə]
positioning	posisjonering (m/f)	[pʉsiʂʉ'neriŋ]
to position (vt)	å posisjonere	[ɔ pʉsiʂʉ'nerə]

price	pris (m)	['pris]
pricing policy	prispolitikk (m)	['pris pʉli'tik]
price formation	prisdannelse (m)	['pris,dɑnəlsə]

77. Advertising

| advertising | reklame (m) | [rɛ'klɑmə] |
| to advertise (vt) | å reklamere | [ɔ rɛklɑ'merə] |

budget	**budsjett** (n)	[bʉd'sɛt]
ad, advertisement	**annonse** (m)	[a'nɔnsə]
TV advertising	**TV-reklame** (m)	['tɛvɛ rɛ'klamə]
radio advertising	**radioreklame** (m)	['radiʉ rɛ'klamə]
outdoor advertising	**utendørsreklame** (m)	['ʉtən͵dœş rɛ'klamə]

mass medias	**massemedier** (n pl)	['masə͵mediər]
periodical (n)	**tidsskrift** (n)	['tid͵skrift]
image (public appearance)	**image** (m)	['imidʒ]

slogan	**slogan** (n)	['slɔgan]
motto (maxim)	**motto** (n)	['mɔtʊ]

campaign	**kampanje** (m)	[kam'panjə]
advertising campaign	**reklamekampanje** (m)	[rɛ'klamə kam'panjə]
target group	**målgruppe** (m/f)	['moːl͵grʉpə]

business card	**visittkort** (n)	[vi'sit͵kɔːt]
leaflet (promotional ~)	**reklameblad** (n)	[rɛ'klamə͵bla]
brochure (e.g. 12 pages ~)	**brosjyre** (m)	[brɔ'şyrə]
pamphlet	**folder** (m)	['fɔlər]
newsletter	**nyhetsbrev** (n)	['nyhets͵brev]

signboard (store sign, etc.)	**skilt** (n)	['şilt]
poster	**plakat, poster** (m)	['pla͵kat], ['pɔstər]
hoarding	**reklameskilt** (m/f)	[rɛ'klamə͵şilt]

78. Banking

bank	**bank** (m)	['bank]
branch (of bank, etc.)	**avdeling** (m)	['av͵deliŋ]

consultant	**konsulent** (m)	[kʊnsʉ'lent]
manager (director)	**forstander** (m)	[fɔ'standər]

bank account	**bankkonto** (m)	['bank͵kɔntʊ]
account number	**kontonummer** (n)	['kɔntʊ͵nʉmər]
current account	**sjekkonto** (m)	['şɛk͵kɔntʊ]
deposit account	**sparekonto** (m)	['sparə͵kɔntʊ]

to open an account	**å åpne en konto**	[ɔ 'ɔpnə en 'kɔntʊ]
to close the account	**å lukke kontoen**	[ɔ 'lʉkə 'kɔntʊən]
to deposit into the account	**å sette inn på kontoen**	[ɔ 'sɛtə in pɔ 'kɔntʊən]
to withdraw (vt)	**å ta ut fra kontoen**	[ɔ 'ta ʉt fra 'kɔntʊən]

deposit	**innskudd** (n)	['in͵skʉd]
to make a deposit	**å sette inn**	[ɔ 'sɛtə in]
wire transfer	**overføring** (m/f)	['ovər͵føriŋ]
to wire, to transfer	**å overføre**	[ɔ 'ovər͵førə]

sum	**sum** (m)	['sʉm]
How much?	**Hvor mye?**	[vʊr 'mye]
signature	**underskrift** (m/f)	['ʉnə͵skrift]
to sign (vt)	**å underskrive**	[ɔ 'ʉnə͵skrivə]

credit card	**kredittkort** (n)	[krɛ'dit̪ˌkɔːt̪]
code (PIN code)	**kode** (m)	['kʊdə]
credit card number	**kreditkortnummer** (n)	[krɛ'dit̪ˌkɔːt̪ 'nʉmər]
cashpoint	**minibank** (m)	['miniˌbank]
cheque	**sjekk** (m)	['ʂɛk]
to write a cheque	**å skrive en sjekk**	[ɔ 'skrivə en 'ʂɛk]
chequebook	**sjekkbok** (m/f)	['ʂɛkˌbʊk]
loan (bank ~)	**lån** (n)	['lɔn]
to apply for a loan	**å søke om lån**	[ɔ ˌsøkə ɔm 'lɔn]
to get a loan	**å få lån**	[ɔ 'fɔ 'lɔn]
to give a loan	**å gi lån**	[ɔ 'ji 'lɔn]
guarantee	**garanti** (m)	[garan'ti]

79. Telephone. Phone conversation

telephone	**telefon** (m)	[tele'fʊn]
mobile phone	**mobiltelefon** (m)	[mʊ'bil tele'fʊn]
answerphone	**telefonsvarer** (m)	[tele'fʊnˌsvarər]
to call (by phone)	**å ringe**	[ɔ 'riŋə]
call, ring	**telefonsamtale** (m)	[tele'fʊn 'samˌtale]
to dial a number	**å slå et nummer**	[ɔ 'ʂlɔ et 'nʉmər]
Hello!	**Hallo!**	[ha'lʊ]
to ask (vt)	**å spørre**	[ɔ 'spøre]
to answer (vi, vt)	**å svare**	[ɔ 'svarə]
to hear (vt)	**å høre**	[ɔ 'hørə]
well (adv)	**godt**	['gɔt]
not well (adv)	**dårlig**	['dɔːli]
noises (interference)	**støy** (m)	['støj]
receiver	**telefonrør** (n)	[tele'fʊnˌrør]
to pick up (~ the phone)	**å ta telefonen**	[ɔ 'ta tele'fʊnən]
to hang up (~ the phone)	**å legge på røret**	[ɔ 'legə pɔ 'rørə]
busy (engaged)	**opptatt**	['ɔpˌtat]
to ring (ab. phone)	**å ringe**	[ɔ 'riŋə]
telephone book	**telefonkatalog** (m)	[tele'fʊn kata'lɔg]
local (adj)	**lokal-**	[lo'kal-]
local call	**lokalsamtale** (m)	[lo'kal 'samˌtale]
trunk (e.g. ~ call)	**riks-**	['riks-]
trunk call	**rikssamtale** (m)	['riks 'samˌtale]
international (adj)	**internasjonal**	['intɛːŋaʂʊˌnal]
international call	**internasjonal samtale** (m)	['intɛːŋaʂʊˌnal 'samˌtale]

80. Mobile telephone

mobile phone	**mobiltelefon** (m)	[mʊ'bil tele'fʊn]
display	**skjerm** (m)	['ʂærm]

| button | knapp (m) | ['knɑp] |
| SIM card | SIM-kort (n) | ['sim‚kɔːt] |

battery	batteri (n)	[batɛ'ri]
to be flat (battery)	å bli utladet	[ɔ 'bli 'ʉt‚ladət]
charger	lader (m)	['lɑdər]

menu	meny (m)	[me'ny]
settings	innstillinger (m/f pl)	['in‚stiliŋər]
tune (melody)	melodi (m)	[melɔ'di]
to select (vt)	å velge	[ɔ 'vɛlgə]

calculator	regnemaskin (m)	['rɛjnə mɑ‚ɕin]
voice mail	telefonsvarer (m)	[tele'fʉn‚svarər]
alarm clock	vekkerklokka (m/f)	['vɛkər‚klɔka]
contacts	kontakter (m pl)	[kʉn'taktər]

| SMS (text message) | SMS-beskjed (m) | [ɛsɛm'ɛs bɛ‚ɕɛ] |
| subscriber | abonnent (m) | [abɔ'nɛnt] |

81. Stationery

| ballpoint pen | kulepenn (m) | ['kʉːlə‚pɛn] |
| fountain pen | fyllepenn (m) | ['fʏlə‚pɛn] |

pencil	blyant (m)	['bly‚ant]
highlighter	merkepenn (m)	['mærkə‚pɛn]
felt-tip pen	tusjpenn (m)	['tʉʂ‚pɛn]

| notepad | notatbok (m/f) | [nʉ'tat‚bʉk] |
| diary | dagbok (m/f) | ['dɑg‚bʉk] |

ruler	linjal (m)	[li'njal]
calculator	regnemaskin (m)	['rɛjnə mɑ‚ɕin]
rubber	viskelær (n)	['viskə‚lær]
drawing pin	tegnestift (m)	['tæjnə‚stift]
paper clip	binders (m)	['bindɛʂ]

glue	lim (n)	['lim]
stapler	stiftemaskin (m)	['stiftə mɑ‚ɕin]
hole punch	hullemaskin (m)	['hʉlə mɑ‚ɕin]
pencil sharpener	blyantspisser (m)	['blyant‚spisər]

82. Kinds of business

accounting services	bokføringstjenester (m pl)	['bʉk‚føriŋs 'tjenɛstər]
advertising	reklame (m)	[rɛ'klamə]
advertising agency	reklamebyrå (n)	[rɛ'klamə by‚ro]
air-conditioners	klimaanlegg (n pl)	['klima'an‚leg]
airline	flyselskap (n)	['flysəl‚skap]
alcoholic beverages	alkoholholdige drikke (m pl)	[alkʉ'hʉl‚hɔldiə 'drikə]
antiques (antique dealers)	antikviteter (m pl)	[antikvi'tetər]

art gallery (contemporary ~)	kunstgalleri (n)	['kʉnstˌgale'ri]
audit services	revisjonstjenester (m pl)	[revi'ʂʉnsˌtjenɛstər]
banking industry	bankvirksomhet (m/f)	['bankˌvirksɔmhet]
beauty salon	skjønnhetssalong (m)	['ʂønhɛts sa'lɔŋ]
bookshop	bokhandel (m)	['bʉkˌhandəl]
brewery	bryggeri (n)	[brʏge'ri]
business centre	forretningssenter (n)	[fɔ'rɛtniŋsˌsɛntər]
business school	handelsskole (m)	['handəlsˌskʉlə]
casino	kasino (n)	[ka'sinʉ]
chemist, pharmacy	apotek (n)	[apʉ'tek]
cinema	kino (m)	['çinʉ]
construction	byggeri (m/f)	[bʏge'ri]
consulting	konsulenttjenester (m pl)	[kʉnsu'lent ˌtjenɛstər]
dental clinic	tannklinik (m)	['tankli'nik]
design	design (m)	['desajn]
dry cleaners	renseri (n)	[rɛnse'ri]
employment agency	rekrutteringsbyrå (n)	['rekrʉˌteriŋs byˌro]
financial services	finansielle tjenester (m pl)	[finan'sielə ˌtjenɛstər]
food products	matvarer (m/f pl)	['matˌvarər]
furniture (e.g. house ~)	møbler (n pl)	['møblər]
clothing, garment	klær (n)	['klær]
hotel	hotell (n)	[hʉ'tɛl]
ice-cream	iskrem (m)	['iskrɛm]
industry (manufacturing)	industri (m)	[indʉ'stri]
insurance	forsikring (m/f)	[fɔ'ʂikriŋ]
Internet	Internett	['intəˌnɛt]
investments (finance)	investering (m/f)	[inve'steriŋ]
jeweller	juveler (m)	[jʉ'velər]
jewellery	smykker (n pl)	['smʏkər]
laundry (shop)	vaskeri (n)	[vaske'ri]
legal adviser	juridisk rådgiver (m pl)	[jʉ'ridisk 'rɔdˌjivər]
light industry	lettindustri (m)	['letˌindʉ'stri]
magazine	magasin, tidsskrift (n)	[maga'sin], ['tidˌskrift]
mail-order selling	postordresalg (m)	['postˌordrə'salg]
medicine	medisin (m)	[medi'sin]
museum	museum (n)	[mʉ'seum]
news agency	nyhetsbyrå (n)	['nyhets byˌro]
newspaper	avis (m/f)	[a'vis]
nightclub	nattklubb (m)	['natˌklʉb]
oil (petroleum)	olje (m)	['ɔljə]
courier services	budtjeneste (m)	[bʉd'tjenɛstə]
pharmaceutics	legemidler (pl)	['legə'midlər]
printing (industry)	trykkeri (n)	[trʏkə'ri]
pub	bar (m)	['bar]
publishing house	forlag (n)	['fɔːˌlag]
radio (~ station)	radio (m)	['radiʉ]
real estate	fast eiendom (m)	[ˌfast 'æjənˌdɔm]

restaurant	**restaurant** (m)	[rɛstʉ'rɑŋ]
security company	**sikkerhetsselskap** (n)	['sikɘrhɛts 'selˌskɑp]
shop	**forretning, butikk** (m)	[fɔ'rɛtniŋ], [bʉ'tik]
sport	**sport, idrett** (m)	['spɔ:t], ['idrɛt]
stock exchange	**børs** (m)	['bœʂ]
supermarket	**supermarked** (n)	['sʉpɘˌmɑrket]
swimming pool (public ~)	**svømmebasseng** (n)	['svœmɘˌbɑ'sɛŋ]
tailor shop	**skredderi** (n)	[skrɛde'ri]
television	**televisjon** (m)	['televiˌʂʊn]
theatre	**teater** (n)	[te'ɑtɘr]
trade (commerce)	**handel** (m)	['hɑndɘl]
transport companies	**transport** (m)	[trɑns'pɔ:t]
travel	**turisme** (m)	[tʉ'rismɘ]
undertakers	**begravelsesbyrå** (n)	[be'grɑvɘlsɘs byˌro]
veterinary surgeon	**dyrlege, veterinær** (m)	['dyrˌlegɘ], [vetɘri'nær]
warehouse	**lager** (n)	['lɑgɘr]
waste collection	**avfallstømming** (m/f)	['ɑvfɑlsˌtœmiŋ]

HUMAN ACTIVITIES

Job. Business. Part 2

83. Show. Exhibition

exhibition, show	messe (m/f)	['mɛsə]
trade show	varemesse (m/f)	['varə‚mɛsə]
participation	deltagelse (m)	['del‚tagəlsə]
to participate (vi)	å delta	[ɔ 'dɛlta]
participant (exhibitor)	deltaker (m)	['del‚takər]
director	direktør (m)	[dirɛk'tør]
organizers' office	arrangørkontor (m)	[araŋ'ʂør kʉn'tʉr]
organizer	arrangør (m)	[araŋ'ʂør]
to organize (vt)	å organisere	[ɔ ɔrgani'serə]
participation form	påmeldingsskjema (n)	['pɔmeliŋs‚ʂɛma]
to fill in (vt)	å utfylle	[ɔ 'ʉt‚fylə]
details	detaljer (m pl)	[de'taljər]
information	informasjon (m)	[informa'ʂʉn]
price (cost, rate)	pris (m)	['pris]
including	inklusive	['inklʉ‚sivə]
to include (vt)	å inkludere	[ɔ inklʉ'derə]
to pay (vi, vt)	å betale	[ɔ be'talə]
registration fee	registreringsavgift (m/f)	[rɛgi'strɛriŋs av'jift]
entrance	inngang (m)	['in‚gaŋ]
pavilion, hall	paviljong (m)	[pavi'ljɔŋ]
to register (vt)	å registrere	[ɔ regi'strerə]
badge (identity tag)	badge (n)	['bædʒ]
stand	messestand (m)	['mɛsə‚stan]
to reserve, to book	å reservere	[ɔ resɛr'verə]
display case	glassmonter (m)	['glas‚mɔntər]
spotlight	lampe (m/f), spotlys (n)	['lampə], ['spɔt‚lys]
design	design (m)	['desajn]
to place (put, set)	å plassere	[ɔ pla'serə]
to be placed	å bli plasseret	[ɔ 'bli pla'serət]
distributor	distributør (m)	[distribʉ'tør]
supplier	leverandør (m)	[levəran'dør]
to supply (vt)	å levere	[ɔ le'verə]
country	land (n)	['lan]
foreign (adj)	utenlandsk	['ʉtən‚lansk]
product	produkt (n)	[prʉ'dʉkt]

association	forening (m/f)	[fɔ'reniŋ]
conference hall	konferansesal (m)	[kʊnfə'rɑnsəˌsɑl]
congress	kongress (m)	[kʊn'grɛs]
contest (competition)	tevling (m)	['tɛvliŋ]

visitor (attendee)	besøkende (m)	[be'søkenə]
to visit (attend)	å besøke	[ɔ be'søkə]
customer	kunde (m)	['kʉndə]

84. Science. Research. Scientists

science	vitenskap (m)	['vitənˌskɑp]
scientific (adj)	vitenskapelig	['vitənˌskɑpəli]
scientist	vitenskapsmann (m)	['vitənˌskɑps mɑn]
theory	teori (m)	[teʊ'ri]

axiom	aksiom (n)	[ɑksi'ɔm]
analysis	analyse (m)	[ɑnɑ'lysə]
to analyse (vt)	å analysere	[ɔ ɑnɑly'serə]
argument (strong ~)	argument (n)	[ɑrgʉ'mɛnt]
substance (matter)	stoff (n), substans (m)	['stɔf], [sʊb'stɑns]

hypothesis	hypotese (m)	[hypʊ'tesə]
dilemma	dilemma (n)	[di'lemɑ]
dissertation	avhandling (m/f)	['ɑvˌhɑndliŋ]
dogma	dogme (n)	['dɔgmə]

doctrine	doktrine (m)	[dɔk'trinə]
research	forskning (m)	['fɔːʂkniŋ]
to research (vt)	å forske	[ɔ 'fɔːʂkə]
tests (laboratory ~)	test (m), prøve (m/f)	['tɛst], ['prøve]
laboratory	laboratorium (n)	[lɑbʊrɑ'tɔrium]

method	metode (m)	[me'tɔdə]
molecule	molekyl (n)	[mʊle'kyl]
monitoring	overvåking (m/f)	['ɔverˌvɔkiŋ]
discovery (act, event)	oppdagelse (m)	['ɔpˌdɑgəlsə]

postulate	postulat (n)	[pɔstʉ'lɑt]
principle	prinsipp (n)	[prin'sip]
forecast	prognose (m)	[prʊg'nʊsə]
to forecast (vt)	å prognostisere	[ɔ prʊgnʊsti'serə]

synthesis	syntese (m)	[sʏn'tesə]
trend (tendency)	tendens (m)	[tɛn'dɛns]
theorem	teorem (n)	[teʊ'rɛm]

teachings	lære (m/f pl)	['lærə]
fact	faktum (n)	['fɑktum]
expedition	ekspedisjon (m)	[ɛkspedi'ʂʊn]
experiment	eksperiment (n)	[ɛksperi'mɛnt]

academician	akademiker (m)	[ɑkɑ'demikər]
bachelor (e.g. ~ of Arts)	bachelor (m)	['bɑtʂɛlɔr]

doctor (PhD)	**doktor** (m)	['dɔktʊr]
Associate Professor	**dosent** (m)	[dʊ'sɛnt]
Master (e.g. ~ of Arts)	**magister** (m)	[mɑ'gistər]
professor	**professor** (m)	[prʊ'fɛsʊr]

Professions and occupations

85. Job search. Dismissal

job	arbeid (n), jobb (m)	['ɑrbæj], ['job]
staff (work force)	ansatte (pl)	['anˌsatə]
personnel	personale (n)	[pæʂʉ'nalə]
career	karriere (m)	[kari'ɛrə]
prospects (chances)	utsikter (m pl)	['ʉtˌsiktər]
skills (mastery)	mesterskap (n)	['mɛstæˌʂkap]
selection (screening)	utvelgelse (m)	['ʉtˌvɛlgəlsə]
employment agency	rekrutteringsbyrå (n)	['rekrʉˌteriŋgs byˌro]
curriculum vitae, CV	CV (m/n)	['sɛvɛ]
job interview	jobbintervju (n)	['job ˌintər'vjʉ]
vacancy	vakanse (m)	['vakansə]
salary, pay	lønn (m/f)	['lœn]
fixed salary	fastlønn (m/f)	['fastˌlœn]
pay, compensation	betaling (m/f)	[be'taliŋ]
position (job)	stilling (m/f)	['stiliŋ]
duty (of employee)	plikt (m/f)	['plikt]
range of duties	arbeidsplikter (m/f pl)	['ɑrbæjdsˌpliktər]
busy (I'm ~)	opptatt	['ɔpˌtat]
to fire (dismiss)	å avskjedige	[ɔ 'afˌʂedigə]
dismissal	avskjedigelse (m)	['afʂeˌdigəlsə]
unemployment	arbeidsløshet (m)	['ɑrbæjdsløsˌhet]
unemployed (n)	arbeidsløs (m)	['ɑrbæjdsˌløs]
retirement	pensjon (m)	[pan'ʂun]
to retire (from job)	å gå av med pensjon	[ɔ 'gɔ ɑ: me pan'ʂun]

86. Business people

director	direktør (m)	[dirɛk'tør]
manager (director)	forstander (m)	[fo'ʂtandər]
boss	boss (m)	['bɔs]
superior	overordnet (m)	['ɔvərˌordnet]
superiors	overordnede (pl)	['ɔvərˌordnedə]
president	president (m)	[prɛsi'dɛnt]
chairman	styreformann (m)	['styrəˌforman]
deputy (substitute)	stedfortreder (m)	['stedfɔːˌtredər]
assistant	assistent (m)	[asi'stɛnt]

| secretary | sekretær (m) | [sɛkrə'tær] |
| personal assistant | privatsekretær (m) | [pri'vɑt sɛkrə'tær] |

businessman	forretningsmann (m)	[fɔ'rɛtniŋs‚mɑn]
entrepreneur	entreprenør (m)	[ɛntreprə'nør]
founder	grunnlegger (m)	['grʉn‚legər]
to found (vt)	å grunnlegge, å stifte	[ɔ 'grʉn‚legə], [ɔ 'stiftə]

founding member	stifter (m)	['stiftər]
partner	partner (m)	['pɑːʈnər]
shareholder	aksjonær (m)	[ɑkʂʉ'nær]

millionaire	millionær (m)	[milju'nær]
billionaire	milliardær (m)	[miljɑː'dær]
owner, proprietor	eier (m)	['æjər]
landowner	jordeier (m)	['juːr‚æjər]

client	kunde (m)	['kʉndə]
regular client	fast kunde (m)	[‚fɑst 'kʉndə]
buyer (customer)	kjøper (m)	['çœːpər]
visitor	besøkende (m)	[be'søkenə]

professional (n)	yrkesmann (m)	['yrkəs‚mɑn]
expert	ekspert (m)	[ɛks'pæːʈ]
specialist	spesialist (m)	[spesiɑ'list]

| banker | bankier (m) | [bɑnki'e] |
| broker | mekler, megler (m) | ['mɛklər] |

cashier	kasserer (m)	[kɑ'serər]
accountant	regnskapsfører (m)	['rɛjnskɑps‚førər]
security guard	sikkerhetsvakt (m/f)	['sikərhɛts‚vɑkt]

investor	investor (m)	[in'vɛstʉr]
debtor	skyldner (m)	['ʂylnər]
creditor	kreditor (m)	['krɛditʉr]
borrower	låntaker (m)	['lɔn‚tɑkər]

| importer | importør (m) | [impɔ:'ʈør] |
| exporter | eksportør (m) | [ɛkspɔ:'ʈør] |

manufacturer	produsent (m)	[prʉdʉ'sɛnt]
distributor	distributør (m)	[distribʉ'tør]
middleman	mellommann (m)	['mɛlɔ‚mɑn]

consultant	konsulent (m)	[kʉnsʉ'lent]
sales representative	representant (m)	[represɛn'tɑnt]
agent	agent (m)	[ɑ'gɛnt]
insurance agent	forsikringsagent (m)	[fɔ'ʂikriŋs ɑ'gɛnt]

87. Service professions

| cook | kokk (m) | ['kʉk] |
| chef (kitchen chef) | sjefkokk (m) | ['ʂɛf‚kʉk] |

baker	baker (m)	['bakər]
barman	bartender (m)	['bɑːˌtɛndər]
waiter	servitør (m)	['særvi'tør]
waitress	servitrise (m/f)	[særvi'trisə]

lawyer, barrister	advokat (m)	[advʊ'kat]
lawyer (legal expert)	jurist (m)	[jʉ'rist]
notary	notar (m)	[nʊ'tar]

electrician	elektriker (m)	[ɛ'lektrikər]
plumber	rørlegger (m)	['rørˌlegər]
carpenter	tømmermann (m)	['tœmərˌman]

masseur	massør (m)	[ma'sør]
masseuse	massøse (m)	[ma'søsə]
doctor	lege (m)	['legə]

taxi driver	taxisjåfør (m)	['taksi ʂɔ'før]
driver	sjåfør (m)	[ʂɔ'før]
delivery man	bud (n)	['bʉd]

chambermaid	stuepike (m/f)	['stʉəˌpikə]
security guard	sikkerhetsvakt (m/f)	['sikərhɛtsˌvakt]
flight attendant (fem.)	flyvertinne (m/f)	[flyvɛ:'ţinə]

schoolteacher	lærer (m)	['lærər]
librarian	bibliotekar (m)	[bibliʊ'tekar]
translator	oversetter (m)	['ɔvəˌʂɛtər]
interpreter	tolk (m)	['tɔlk]
guide	guide (m)	['gajd]

hairdresser	frisør (m)	[fri'sør]
postman	postbud (n)	['pɔstˌbʉd]
salesman (store staff)	forselger (m)	[fɔ'ʂɛlər]

gardener	gartner (m)	['gaːţnər]
domestic servant	tjener (m)	['tjenər]
maid (female servant)	tjenestepike (m/f)	['tjenɛstəˌpikə]
cleaner (cleaning lady)	vaskedame (m/f)	['vaskəˌdamə]

88. Military professions and ranks

private	menig (m)	['meni]
sergeant	sersjant (m)	[sær'ʂant]
lieutenant	løytnant (m)	['løjtˌnant]
captain	kaptein (m)	[kap'tæjn]

major	major (m)	[ma'jɔr]
colonel	oberst (m)	['ʊbɛʂt]
general	general (m)	[gene'ral]
marshal	marskalk (m)	['marʂal]
admiral	admiral (m)	[admi'ral]
military (n)	militær (m)	[mili'tær]
soldier	soldat (m)	[sʊl'dat]

| officer | offiser (m) | [ɔfi'sɛr] |
| commander | befalshaver (m) | [be'fals‚havər] |

border guard	grensevakt (m/f)	['grɛnsə‚vakt]
radio operator	radiooperatør (m)	['radiʊ ʊpəra'tør]
scout (searcher)	oppklaringssoldat (m)	['ɔp‚klariŋ sʊl'dat]
pioneer (sapper)	pioner (m)	[piʊ'ner]
marksman	skytter (m)	['ʂytər]
navigator	styrmann (m)	['styr‚man]

89. Officials. Priests

| king | konge (m) | ['kʊŋə] |
| queen | dronning (m/f) | ['drɔniŋ] |

| prince | prins (m) | ['prins] |
| princess | prinsesse (m/f) | [prin'sɛsə] |

| czar | tsar (m) | ['tsɑr] |
| czarina | tsarina (m) | [tsɑ'rinɑ] |

president	president (m)	[prɛsi'dɛnt]
Secretary (minister)	minister (m)	[mi'nistər]
prime minister	statsminister (m)	['stɑts mi'nistər]
senator	senator (m)	[se'nɑtʊr]

diplomat	diplomat (m)	[diplʊ'mɑt]
consul	konsul (m)	['kʊn‚sʉl]
ambassador	ambassadør (m)	[ɑmbɑsɑ'dør]
counsillor (diplomatic officer)	rådgiver (m)	['rɔdjivər]

official, functionary (civil servant)	embetsmann (m)	['ɛmbets‚mɑn]
prefect	prefekt (m)	[prɛ'fɛkt]
mayor	borgermester (m)	[bɔrgər'mɛstər]
judge	dommer (m)	['dɔmər]
prosecutor	anklager (m)	['ɑn‚klɑgər]

missionary	misjonær (m)	[miʂʊ'nær]
monk	munk (m)	['mʉnk]
abbot	abbed (m)	['ɑbed]
rabbi	rabbiner (m)	[rɑ'binər]

vizier	vesir (m)	[vɛ'sir]
shah	sjah (m)	['ʂɑ]
sheikh	sjeik (m)	['ʂæjk]

90. Agricultural professions

beekeeper	birøkter (m)	['bi‚røktər]
shepherd	gjeter, hyrde (m)	['jetər], ['hyrdə]
agronomist	agronom (m)	[ɑgrʊ'nʊm]

| cattle breeder | husdyrholder (m) | ['hʉsdyr,hɔldər] |
| veterinary surgeon | dyrlege, veterinær (m) | ['dyr,legə], [vetəri'nær] |

farmer	gårdbruker, bonde (m)	['gɔːr,brʉkər], ['bɔnə]
winemaker	vinmaker (m)	['vin,makər]
zoologist	zoolog (m)	[sʉː'lɔg]
cowboy	cowboy (m)	['kaw,bɔj]

91. Art professions

| actor | skuespiller (m) | ['skʉə,spilər] |
| actress | skuespillerinne (m/f) | ['skʉə,spilə'rinə] |

| singer (masc.) | sanger (m) | ['saŋər] |
| singer (fem.) | sangerinne (m/f) | [saŋə'rinə] |

| dancer (masc.) | danser (m) | ['dansər] |
| dancer (fem.) | danserinne (m/f) | [danse'rinə] |

| performer (masc.) | skuespiller (m) | ['skʉə,spilər] |
| performer (fem.) | skuespillerinne (m/f) | ['skʉə,spilə'rinə] |

musician	musiker (m)	['mʉsikər]
pianist	pianist (m)	[pia'nist]
guitar player	gitarspiller (m)	[gi'tar,spilər]

conductor (orchestra ~)	dirigent (m)	[diri'gɛnt]
composer	komponist (m)	[kʉmpʉ'nist]
impresario	impresario (m)	[impre'sariʉ]

film director	regissør (m)	[rɛʂi'sør]
producer	produsent (m)	[prʉdʉ'sɛnt]
scriptwriter	manusforfatter (m)	['manʉs fɔr'fatər]
critic	kritiker (m)	['kritikər]

writer	forfatter (m)	[fɔr'fatər]
poet	poet, dikter (m)	['pɔɛt], ['diktər]
sculptor	skulptør (m)	[skʉlp'tør]
artist (painter)	kunstner (m)	['kʉnstnər]

juggler	sjonglør (m)	[ʂɔŋ'lør]
clown	klovn (m)	['klɔvn]
acrobat	akrobat (m)	[akrʉ'bat]
magician	tryllekunstner (m)	['trʏlə,kʉnstnər]

92. Various professions

doctor	lege (m)	['legə]
nurse	sykepleierske (m/f)	['sykə,plæjeʂkə]
psychiatrist	psykiater (m)	[syki'atər]
dentist	tannlege (m)	['tan,legə]
surgeon	kirurg (m)	[çi'rʉrg]

astronaut	astronaut (m)	[astrʊ'naʊt]
astronomer	astronom (m)	[astrʊ'nʊm]

driver (of taxi, etc.)	fører (m)	['fører]
train driver	lokfører (m)	['lʊk‚fører]
mechanic	mekaniker (m)	[me'kaniker]

miner	gruvearbeider (m)	['grʉvə'ar‚bæjder]
worker	arbeider (m)	['ar‚bæjder]
locksmith	låsesmed (m)	['loːsə‚sme]
joiner (carpenter)	snekker (m)	['snɛker]
turner (lathe machine operator)	dreier (m)	['dræjer]
building worker	bygningsarbeider (m)	['bʏgniŋs 'ar‚bæjer]
welder	sveiser (m)	['svæjser]

professor (title)	professor (m)	[prʊ'fɛsʊr]
architect	arkitekt (m)	[arki'tɛkt]
historian	historiker (m)	[hi'stʊriker]
scientist	vitenskapsmann (m)	['viten‚skaps man]
physicist	fysiker (m)	['fysiker]
chemist (scientist)	kjemiker (m)	['çemiker]

archaeologist	arkeolog (m)	[‚arkeʊ'lɔg]
geologist	geolog (m)	[geʊ'lɔg]
researcher (scientist)	forsker (m)	['fɔʂker]

babysitter	babysitter (m)	['bɛby‚siter]
teacher, educator	lærer, pedagog (m)	[lærer], [peda'gɔg]

editor	redaktør (m)	[rɛdak'tør]
editor-in-chief	sjefredaktør (m)	['ʂɛf rɛdak'tør]
correspondent	korrespondent (m)	[kʊrespon'dɛnt]
typist (fem.)	maskinskriverske (m)	[ma'ʂin ‚skrivɛʂkə]

designer	designer (m)	[de'sajner]
computer expert	dataekspert (m)	['data ɛks'pɛːt]
programmer	programmerer (m)	[prʊgra'merer]
engineer (designer)	ingeniør (m)	[inʂə'njør]

sailor	sjømann (m)	['ʂø‚man]
seaman	matros (m)	[ma'trʊs]
rescuer	redningsmann (m)	['rɛdniŋs‚man]
firefighter	brannmann (m)	['bran‚man]
police officer	politi (m)	[pʊli'ti]
watchman	nattvakt (m)	['nat‚vakt]
detective	detektiv (m)	[detɛk'tiv]

customs officer	tollbetjent (m)	['tɔlbe‚tjɛnt]
bodyguard	livvakt (m/f)	['liv‚vakt]
prison officer	fangevokter (m)	['faŋe‚vokter]
inspector	inspektør (m)	[inspɛk'tør]

sportsman	idrettsmann (m)	['idrɛts‚man]
trainer, coach	trener (m)	['trener]
butcher	slakter (m)	['ʂlakter]

cobbler (shoe repairer)	skomaker (m)	['skʊˌmɑkər]
merchant	handelsmann (m)	['hɑndəlsˌmɑn]
loader (person)	lastearbeider (m)	['lɑstə'ɑrˌbæjdər]

fashion designer	moteskaper (m)	['mʊtəˌskɑpər]
model (fem.)	modell (m)	[mʊ'dɛl]

93. Occupations. Social status

schoolboy	skolegutt (m)	['skʊləˌgʉt]
student (college ~)	student (m)	[stʉ'dɛnt]

philosopher	filosof (m)	[filu'sʊf]
economist	økonom (m)	[økʊ'nʊm]
inventor	oppfinner (m)	['ɔpˌfinər]

unemployed (n)	arbeidsløs (m)	['ɑrbæjdsˌløs]
pensioner	pensjonist (m)	[panʂʊ'nist]
spy, secret agent	spion (m)	[spi'un]

prisoner	fange (m)	['fɑŋə]
striker	streiker (m)	['stræjkər]
bureaucrat	byråkrat (m)	[byrɔ'krɑt]
traveller (globetrotter)	reisende (m)	['ræjsenə]

gay, homosexual (n)	homofil (m)	['hʊmʊˌfil]
hacker	hacker (m)	['hakər]
hippie	hippie (m)	['hipi]

bandit	banditt (m)	[bɑn'dit]
hit man, killer	leiemorder (m)	['læjəˌmʊrdər]
drug addict	narkoman (m)	[nɑrkʊ'mɑn]
drug dealer	narkolanger (m)	['nɑrkɔˌlɑŋər]
prostitute (fem.)	prostituert (m)	[prʊstitʉ'e:t]
pimp	hallik (m)	['hɑlik]

sorcerer	trollmann (m)	['trɔlˌmɑn]
sorceress (evil ~)	trollkjerring (m/f)	['trɔlˌçæriŋ]
pirate	pirat, sjørøver (m)	['pi'rɑt], ['ʂøˌrøvər]
slave	slave (m)	['slɑvə]
samurai	samurai (m)	[sɑmʉ'rɑj]
savage (primitive)	villmann (m)	['vilˌmɑn]

Education

94. School

school	skole (m/f)	['skʉlə]
headmaster	rektor (m)	['rektʉr]
pupil (boy)	elev (m)	[e'lev]
pupil (girl)	elev (m)	[e'lev]
schoolboy	skolegutt (m)	['skʉlə,gʉt]
schoolgirl	skolepike (m)	['skʉlə,pikə]
to teach (sb)	å undervise	[ɔ 'ʉnərˌvisə]
to learn (language, etc.)	å lære	[ɔ 'lærə]
to learn by heart	å lære utenat	[ɔ 'lærə 'ʉtənat]
to learn (~ to count, etc.)	å lære	[ɔ 'lærə]
to be at school	å gå på skolen	[ɔ 'gɔ pɔ 'skʉlən]
to go to school	å gå på skolen	[ɔ 'gɔ pɔ 'skʉlən]
alphabet	alfabet (n)	[alfɑ'bet]
subject (at school)	fag (n)	['fɑg]
classroom	klasserom (m/f)	['klɑsəˌrʉm]
lesson	time (m)	['timə]
playtime, break	frikvarter (n)	['frikvɑːˌʈər]
school bell	skoleklokke (m/f)	['skʉləˌklɔkə]
school desk	skolepult (m)	['skʉləˌpʉlt]
blackboard	tavle (m/f)	['tɑvlə]
mark	karakter (m)	[karak'ter]
good mark	god karakter (m)	['gʉ karak'ter]
bad mark	dårlig karakter (m)	['doː[i karak'ter]
to give a mark	å gi en karakter	[ɔ 'ji en karak'ter]
mistake, error	feil (m)	['fæjl]
to make mistakes	å gjøre feil	[ɔ 'jørə ˌfæjl]
to correct (an error)	å rette	[ɔ 'rɛtə]
crib	fuskelapp (m)	['fʉskəˌlap]
homework	lekser (m/f pl)	['leksər]
exercise (in education)	øvelse (m)	['øvəlsə]
to be present	å være til stede	[ɔ 'værə til 'stedə]
to be absent	å være fraværende	[ɔ 'værə 'frɑˌværənə]
to miss school	å skulke skolen	[ɔ 'skʉlkə 'skʉlən]
to punish (vt)	å straffe	[ɔ 'strafə]
punishment	straff, avstraffelse (m)	['straf], ['afˌstrafəlsə]
conduct (behaviour)	oppførsel (m)	['ɔpˌfœʂəl]

school report	karakterbok (m/f)	[karak'ter,bʊk]
pencil	blyant (m)	['bly,ant]
rubber	viskelær (n)	['viskə,lær]
chalk	kritt (n)	['krit]
pencil case	pennal (n)	[pɛ'nal]
schoolbag	skoleveske (m/f)	['skʊlə,vɛskə]
pen	penn (m)	['pɛn]
exercise book	skrivebok (m/f)	['skrivə,bʊk]
textbook	lærebok (m/f)	['lærə,bʊk]
compasses	passer (m)	['pasər]
to make technical drawings	å tegne	[ɔ 'tæjnə]
technical drawing	teknisk tegning (m/f)	['tɛknisk ,tæjniŋ]
poem	dikt (n)	['dikt]
by heart (adv)	utenat	['ʉtən,at]
to learn by heart	å lære utenat	[ɔ 'lærə 'ʉtənat]
school holidays	skoleferie (m)	['skʊlə,fɛriə]
to be on holiday	å være på ferie	[ɔ 'værə pɔ 'fɛriə]
to spend holidays	å tilbringe ferien	[ɔ 'til,briŋə 'fɛriən]
test (at school)	prøve (m/f)	['prøvə]
essay (composition)	essay (n)	[ɛ'sɛj]
dictation	diktat (m)	[dik'tat]
exam (examination)	eksamen (m)	[ɛk'samən]
to do an exam	å ta eksamen	[ɔ 'ta ɛk'samən]
experiment (e.g., chemistry ~)	forsøk (n)	['fɔ'søk]

95. College. University

academy	akademi (n)	[akade'mi]
university	universitet (n)	[ʉnivæʂi'tet]
faculty (e.g., ~ of Medicine)	fakultet (n)	[fakʉl'tet]
student (masc.)	student (m)	[stʉ'dɛnt]
student (fem.)	kvinnelig student (m)	['kvinəli stʉ'dɛnt]
lecturer (teacher)	lærer, foreleser (m)	['lærər], ['fʊrə,lesər]
lecture hall, room	auditorium (n)	[,aʊdi'tʊrium]
graduate	alumn (m)	[a'lʉmn]
diploma	diplom (n)	[di'plʊm]
dissertation	avhandling (m/f)	['av,handliŋ]
study (report)	studie (m)	['stʉdiə]
laboratory	laboratorium (n)	[labʊra'tɔrium]
lecture	forelesning (m)	['fɔrə,lesniŋ]
coursemate	studiekamerat (m)	['stʉdiə kame,rat]
scholarship, bursary	stipendium (n)	[sti'pɛndium]
academic degree	akademisk grad (m)	[aka'demisk ,grad]

96. Sciences. Disciplines

mathematics	matematikk (m)	[matəma'tik]
algebra	algebra (m)	['algə,bra]
geometry	geometri (m)	[geʊme'tri]
astronomy	astronomi (m)	[astrʊnʊ'mi]
biology	biologi (m)	[biʊlʊ'gi]
geography	geografi (m)	[geʊgra'fi]
geology	geologi (m)	[geʊlʊ'gi]
history	historie (m/f)	[hi'stʊriə]
medicine	medisin (m)	[medi'sin]
pedagogy	pedagogikk (m)	[pedagʊ'gik]
law	rett (m)	['rɛt]
physics	fysikk (m)	[fy'sik]
chemistry	kjemi (m)	[çe'mi]
philosophy	filosofi (m)	[filʊsʊ'fi]
psychology	psykologi (m)	[sikʊlʊ'gi]

97. Writing system. Orthography

grammar	grammatikk (m)	[grama'tik]
vocabulary	ordforråd (n)	['u:rfʊ,rɔd]
phonetics	fonetikk (m)	[fʊne'tik]
noun	substantiv (n)	['sʊbstan,tiv]
adjective	adjektiv (n)	['adjɛk,tiv]
verb	verb (n)	['værb]
adverb	adverb (n)	[ad'væ:b]
pronoun	pronomen (n)	[prʊ'nʊmən]
interjection	interjeksjon (m)	[interjɛk'ʂʊn]
preposition	preposisjon (m)	[prɛpʊsi'ʂʊn]
root	rot (m/f)	['rʊt]
ending	endelse (m)	['ɛnəlsə]
prefix	prefiks (n)	[prɛ'fiks]
syllable	stavelse (m)	['stavəlsə]
suffix	suffiks (n)	[sʊ'fiks]
stress mark	betoning (m), trykk (n)	['be'tɔniŋ], ['trʏk]
apostrophe	apostrof (m)	[apʊ'strɔf]
full stop	punktum (n)	['pʊnktum]
comma	komma (n)	['kɔma]
semicolon	semikolon (n)	[,semikʊ'lɔn]
colon	kolon (n)	['kʊlɔn]
ellipsis	tre prikker (m pl)	['tre 'prikər]
question mark	spørsmålstegn (n)	['spœʂmols,tæjn]
exclamation mark	utropstegn (n)	['ʉtrʊps,tæjn]

inverted commas	anførselstegn (n pl)	[ɑnˈfœʂɛlsˌtejn]
in inverted commas	i anførselstegn	[i ɑnˈfœʂɛlsˌtejn]
parenthesis	parentes (m)	[pɑrɛnˈtes]
in parenthesis	i parentes	[i pɑrɛnˈtes]

hyphen	bindestrek (m)	[ˈbinəˌstrek]
dash	tankestrek (m)	[ˈtɑnkəˌstrek]
space (between words)	mellomrom (n)	[ˈmɛlɔmˌrʊm]

| letter | bokstav (m) | [ˈbʊkstɑv] |
| capital letter | stor bokstav (m) | [ˈstʊr ˈbʊkstɑv] |

| vowel (n) | vokal (m) | [vʊˈkɑl] |
| consonant (n) | konsonant (m) | [kʊnsʊˈnɑnt] |

sentence	setning (m)	[ˈsɛtniŋ]
subject	subjekt (n)	[sʉbˈjɛkt]
predicate	predikat (n)	[prɛdiˈkɑt]

line	linje (m)	[ˈlinjə]
on a new line	på ny linje	[pɔ ny ˈlinjə]
paragraph	avsnitt (n)	[ˈɑfˌsnit]

word	ord (n)	[ˈuːr]
group of words	ordgruppe (m/f)	[ˈuːrˌgrʉpə]
expression	uttrykk (n)	[ˈʉtˌtrʏk]
synonym	synonym (n)	[synʊˈnym]
antonym	antonym (n)	[ɑntʉˈnym]

rule	regel (m)	[ˈrɛgəl]
exception	unntak (n)	[ˈʉnˌtɑk]
correct (adj)	riktig	[ˈrikti]

conjugation	bøyning (m/f)	[ˈbøjniŋ]
declension	bøyning (m/f)	[ˈbøjniŋ]
nominal case	kasus (m)	[ˈkɑsʉs]
question	spørsmål (n)	[ˈspœʂˌmol]
to underline (vt)	å understreke	[ɔ ˈʉnəˌstrekə]
dotted line	prikket linje (m)	[ˈprikət ˈlinjə]

98. Foreign languages

language	språk (n)	[ˈsprɔk]
foreign (adj)	fremmed-	[ˈfremə-]
foreign language	fremmedspråk (n)	[ˈfremedˌsprɔk]
to study (vt)	å studere	[ɔ stʉˈderə]
to learn (language, etc.)	å lære	[ɔ ˈlærə]

to read (vi, vt)	å lese	[ɔ ˈlesə]
to speak (vi, vt)	å tale	[ɔ ˈtalə]
to understand (vt)	å forstå	[ɔ fɔˈstɔ]
to write (vt)	å skrive	[ɔ ˈskrivə]
fast (adv)	fort	[ˈfʊːʈ]
slowly (adv)	langsomt	[ˈlɑŋsɔmt]

fluently (adv)	flytende	['flytnə]
rules	regler (m pl)	['rɛglər]
grammar	grammatikk (m)	[gramɑ'tik]
vocabulary	ordforråd (n)	['uːrfʊˌrɔd]
phonetics	fonetikk (m)	[fʊne'tik]
textbook	lærebok (m/f)	['læːrəˌbʊk]
dictionary	ordbok (m/f)	['uːrˌbʊk]
teach-yourself book	lærebok (m/f) for selvstudium	['læːrəˌbʊk fɔ 'selˌstʉdium]
phrasebook	parlør (m)	[pɑː'ɭør]
cassette, tape	kassett (m)	[kɑ'sɛt]
videotape	videokassett (m)	['videʊ kɑ'sɛt]
CD, compact disc	CD-rom (m)	['sɛdɛˌrʊm]
DVD	DVD (m)	[deve'de]
alphabet	alfabet (n)	[alfɑ'bet]
to spell (vt)	å stave	[ɔ 'stɑvə]
pronunciation	uttale (m)	['ʉtˌtalə]
accent	aksent (m)	[ak'sɑŋ]
with an accent	med aksent	[me ak'sɑŋ]
without an accent	uten aksent	['ʉtən ak'sɑŋ]
word	ord (n)	['uːr]
meaning	betydning (m)	[be'tʏdniŋ]
course (e.g. a French ~)	kurs (n)	['kʉs]
to sign up	å anmelde seg	[ɔ 'anˌmɛlə sæj]
teacher	lærer (m)	['læːrər]
translation (process)	oversettelse (m)	['ɔvəˌsɛtəlsə]
translation (text, etc.)	oversettelse (m)	['ɔvəˌsɛtəlsə]
translator	oversetter (m)	['ɔvəˌsɛtər]
interpreter	tolk (m)	['tɔlk]
polyglot	polyglott (m)	[pʊlʏ'glɔt]
memory	minne (n), hukommelse (m)	['minə], [hʉ'kɔməlsə]

Rest. Entertainment. Travel

99. Trip. Travel

tourism, travel	turisme (m)	[tʉ'rismə]
tourist	turist (m)	[tʉ'rist]
trip, voyage	reise (m/f)	['ræjsə]
adventure	eventyr (n)	['ɛvənˌtyr]
trip, journey	tripp (m)	['trip]
holiday	ferie (m)	['fɛriə]
to be on holiday	å være på ferie	[ɔ 'værə pɔ 'fɛriə]
rest	hvile (m/f)	['vilə]
train	tog (n)	['tɔg]
by train	med tog	[me 'tɔg]
aeroplane	fly (n)	['fly]
by aeroplane	med fly	[me 'fly]
by car	med bil	[me 'bil]
by ship	med skip	[me 'şip]
luggage	bagasje (m)	[ba'gaşə]
suitcase	koffert (m)	['kʊfɛːt]
luggage trolley	bagasjetralle (m/f)	[ba'gaşəˌtralə]
passport	pass (n)	['pas]
visa	visum (n)	['visʉm]
ticket	billett (m)	[bi'let]
air ticket	flybillett (m)	['fly bi'let]
guidebook	reisehåndbok (m/f)	['ræjsəˌhonbʊk]
map (tourist ~)	kart (n)	['kaːt]
area (rural ~)	område (n)	['ɔmˌroːdə]
place, site	sted (n)	['sted]
exotic (adj)	eksotisk	[ɛk'sʊtisk]
amazing (adj)	forunderlig	[fɔ'rʉndeːli]
group	gruppe (m)	['grʉpə]
excursion, sightseeing tour	utflukt (m/f)	['ʉtˌflʉkt]
guide (person)	guide (m)	['gajd]

100. Hotel

hotel	hotell (n)	[hʊ'tɛl]
motel	motell (n)	[mʊ'tɛl]
three-star (~ hotel)	trestjernet	['treˌstjæːnə]
five-star	femstjernet	['fɛmˌstjæːnə]

to stay (in a hotel, etc.)	å bo	[ɔ 'bʊ]
room	rom (n)	['rʊm]
single room	enkeltrom (n)	['ɛnkelt‚rʊm]
double room	dobbeltrom (n)	['dɔbəlt‚rʊm]
to book a room	å reservere rom	[ɔ resɛr'verə 'rʊm]
half board	halvpensjon (m)	['hɑl pɑn‚sʊn]
full board	fullpensjon (m)	['fʉl pɑn‚sʊn]
with bath	med badekar	[me 'bɑdə‚kɑr]
with shower	med dusj	[me 'dʉʂ]
satellite television	satellitt-TV (m)	[sɑtɛ'lit 'tɛvɛ]
air-conditioner	klimaanlegg (n)	['klimɑ'ɑn‚leg]
towel	håndkle (n)	['hɔn‚kle]
key	nøkkel (m)	['nøkəl]
administrator	administrator (m)	[admini'strɑ:tʊr]
chambermaid	stuepike (m/f)	['stʉə‚pikə]
porter	pikkolo (m)	['pikɔlɔ]
doorman	portier (m)	[pɔ:'tje]
restaurant	restaurant (m)	[rɛstʉ'rɑŋ]
pub, bar	bar (m)	['bɑr]
breakfast	frokost (m)	['frʊkɔst]
dinner	middag (m)	['mi‚dɑ]
buffet	buffet (m)	[bʉ'fɛ]
lobby	hall, lobby (m)	['hɑl], ['lɔbi]
lift	heis (m)	['hæjs]
DO NOT DISTURB	VENNLIGST IKKE FORSTYRR!	['vɛnligt ikə fo'ʂtyr]
NO SMOKING	RØYKING FORBUDT	['røjkiŋ for'bʉt]

Technical equipment

101. Computer

computer	datamaskin (m)	['data maˌʂin]
notebook, laptop	bærbar, laptop (m)	['bærˌbar], ['laptɔp]
to turn on	å slå på	[ɔ 'ʂlɔ pɔ]
to turn off	å slå av	[ɔ 'ʂlɔ ɑː]
keyboard	tastatur (n)	[tastɑ'tʉr]
key	tast (m)	['tast]
mouse	mus (m/f)	['mʉs]
mouse mat	musematte (m/f)	['mʉseˌmate]
button	knapp (m)	['knɑp]
cursor	markør (m)	[mɑr'kør]
monitor	monitor (m)	['mɔnitɔr]
screen	skjerm (m)	['ʂærm]
hard disk	harddisk (m)	['harˌdisk]
hard disk capacity	harddiskkapasitet (m)	['harˌdisk kɑpɑsi'tet]
memory	minne (n)	['mine]
random access memory	hovedminne (n)	['hɔvedˌmine]
file	fil (m)	['fil]
folder	mappe (m/f)	['mape]
to open (vt)	å åpne	[ɔ 'ɔpne]
to close (vt)	å lukke	[ɔ 'lʉke]
to save (vt)	å lagre	[ɔ 'lagre]
to delete (vt)	å slette, å fjerne	[ɔ 'ʂlete], [ɔ 'fjæːŋe]
to copy (vt)	å kopiere	[ɔ kʉ'pjere]
to sort (vt)	å sortere	[ɔ sɔː'tere]
to transfer (copy)	å overføre	[ɔ 'ɔverˌføre]
programme	program (n)	[prʉ'gram]
software	programvare (m/f)	[prʉ'gramˌvare]
programmer	programmerer (m)	[prʉgrɑ'merer]
to program (vt)	å programmere	[ɔ prʉgrɑ'mere]
hacker	hacker (m)	['haker]
password	passord (n)	['pasˌuːr]
virus	virus (m)	['virʉs]
to find, to detect	å oppdage	[ɔ 'ɔpˌdage]
byte	byte (m)	['bajt]
megabyte	megabyte (m)	['megaˌbajt]
data	data (m pl)	['data]

database	database (m)	['dɑtɑˌbɑsə]
cable (USB, etc.)	kabel (m)	['kɑbəl]
to disconnect (vt)	å koble fra	[ɔ 'kɔblə frɑ]
to connect (sth to sth)	å koble	[ɔ 'kɔblə]

102. Internet. E-mail

Internet	Internett	['intəˌnɛt]
browser	nettleser (m)	['nɛtˌlesər]
search engine	søkemotor (m)	['søkəˌmɔtʉr]
provider	leverandør (m)	[levərɑn'dør]
webmaster	webmaster (m)	['vɛbˌmɑstər]
website	webside, hjemmeside (m/f)	['vɛbˌsidə], ['jɛməˌsidə]
webpage	nettside (m)	['nɛtˌsidə]
address (e-mail ~)	adresse (m)	[ɑ'drɛsə]
address book	adressebok (f)	[ɑ'drɛsəˌbʉk]
postbox	postkasse (m/f)	['pɔstˌkɑsə]
post	post (m)	['pɔst]
full (adj)	full	['fʉl]
message	melding (m/f)	['mɛliŋ]
incoming messages	innkommende meldinger	['inˌkɔmənə 'mɛliŋər]
outgoing messages	utgående meldinger	['ʉtˌgɔənə 'mɛliŋər]
sender	avsender (m)	['ɑfˌsɛnər]
to send (vt)	å sende	[ɔ 'sɛnə]
sending (of mail)	avsending (m)	['ɑfˌsɛniŋ]
receiver	mottaker (m)	['mɔtˌtɑkər]
to receive (vt)	å motta	[ɔ 'mɔtɑ]
correspondence	korrespondanse (m)	[kʉrespɔn'dɑnsə]
to correspond (vi)	å brevveksle	[ɔ 'brɛvˌvɛkslə]
file	fil (m)	['fil]
to download (vt)	å laste ned	[ɔ 'lɑstə 'ne]
to create (vt)	å opprette	[ɔ 'ɔpˌrɛtə]
to delete (vt)	å slette, å fjerne	[ɔ 'ʂlɛtə], [ɔ 'fjæ:ɳə]
deleted (adj)	slettet	['ʂlɛtət]
connection (ADSL, etc.)	forbindelse (m)	[fɔr'binəlsə]
speed	hastighet (m/f)	['hɑstiˌhet]
modem	modem (n)	['mʉ'dɛm]
access	tilgang (m)	['tilˌgɑŋ]
port (e.g. input ~)	port (m)	['pɔ:t]
connection (make a ~)	tilkobling (m/f)	['tilˌkɔbliŋ]
to connect to ... (vi)	å koble	[ɔ 'kɔblə]
to select (vt)	å velge	[ɔ 'vɛlgə]
to search (for ...)	å søke etter ...	[ɔ 'søkə ˌɛtər ...]

103. Electricity

electricity	elektrisitet (m)	[ɛlektrɪsɪˈtet]
electric, electrical (adj)	elektrisk	[ɛˈlektrisk]
electric power station	kraftverk (n)	[ˈkrɑftˌværk]
energy	energi (m)	[ɛnærˈgi]
electric power	elkraft (m/f)	[ˈɛlˌkrɑft]
light bulb	lyspære (m/f)	[ˈlysˌpærə]
torch	lommelykt (m/f)	[ˈlʊməˌlʏkt]
street light	gatelykt (m/f)	[ˈgɑtəˌlʏkt]
light	lys (n)	[ˈlys]
to turn on	å slå på	[ɔ ˈslɔ pɔ]
to turn off	å slå av	[ɔ ˈslɔ ɑː]
to turn off the light	å slokke lyset	[ɔ ˈslɔkə ˈlysə]
to burn out (vi)	å brenne ut	[ɔ ˈbrɛnə ʉt]
short circuit	kortslutning (m)	[ˈkuːʈˌslʉtnɪŋ]
broken wire	kabelbrudd (n)	[ˈkɑbəlˌbrʉd]
contact (electrical ~)	kontakt (m)	[kʊnˈtɑkt]
light switch	strømbryter (m)	[ˈstrømˌbrytər]
socket outlet	stikkontakt (m)	[ˈstik kʊnˌtɑkt]
plug	støpsel (n)	[ˈstøpsəl]
extension lead	skjøteledning (m)	[ˈʂøtəˌlednɪŋ]
fuse	sikring (m)	[ˈsikrɪŋ]
cable, wire	ledning (m)	[ˈlednɪŋ]
wiring	ledningsnett (n)	[ˈlednɪŋsˌnɛt]
ampere	ampere (m)	[amˈpɛr]
amperage	strømstyrke (m)	[ˈstrømˌstyrkə]
volt	volt (m)	[ˈvɔlt]
voltage	spenning (m/f)	[ˈspɛnɪŋ]
electrical device	elektrisk apparat (n)	[ɛˈlektrisk ɑpɑˈrɑt]
indicator	indikator (m)	[indiˈkɑtʊr]
electrician	elektriker (m)	[ɛˈlektrikər]
to solder (vt)	å lodde	[ɔ ˈlɔdə]
soldering iron	loddebolt (m)	[ˈlɔdəˌbolt]
electric current	strøm (m)	[ˈstrøm]

104. Tools

tool, instrument	verktøy (n)	[ˈværkˌtøj]
tools	verktøy (n pl)	[ˈværkˌtøj]
equipment (factory ~)	utstyr (n)	[ˈʉtˌstyr]
hammer	hammer (m)	[ˈhɑmər]
screwdriver	skrutrekker (m)	[ˈskrʉˌtrɛkər]
axe	øks (m/f)	[ˈøks]

saw	sag (m/f)	['sɑg]
to saw (vt)	å sage	[ɔ 'sɑgə]
plane (tool)	høvel (m)	['høvəl]
to plane (vt)	å høvle	[ɔ 'høvlə]
soldering iron	loddebolt (m)	['lɔdə‚bɔlt]
to solder (vt)	å lodde	[ɔ 'lɔdə]

file (tool)	fil (m/f)	['fil]
carpenter pincers	knipetang (m/f)	['knipə‚tɑŋ]
combination pliers	flattang (m/f)	['flɑt‚tɑŋ]
chisel	hoggjern, huggjern (n)	['hʊg‚jæːɳ]

drill bit	bor (m/n)	['bʊr]
electric drill	boremaskin (m)	['bɔre mɑ‚ʂin]
to drill (vi, vt)	å bore	[ɔ 'bɔrə]

knife	kniv (m)	['kniv]
pocket knife	lommekniv (m)	['lʊmə‚kniv]
folding (~ knife)	folde-	['fɔlə-]
blade	blad (n)	['blɑ]

sharp (blade, etc.)	skarp	['skɑrp]
dull, blunt (adj)	sløv	['sløv]
to get blunt (dull)	å bli sløv	[ɔ 'bli 'sløv]
to sharpen (vt)	å skjerpe, å slipe	[ɔ 'ʂɛrpə], [ɔ 'ʂlipə]

bolt	bolt (m)	['bɔlt]
nut	mutter (m)	['mʉtər]
thread (of a screw)	gjenge (n)	['jɛŋə]
wood screw	skrue (m)	['skrʉə]

nail	spiker (m)	['spikər]
nailhead	spikerhode (n)	['spikər‚hʊdə]

ruler (for measuring)	linjal (m)	[li'njɑl]
tape measure	målebånd (n)	['moːlə‚bɔn]
spirit level	vater, vaterpass (n)	['vɑtər], ['vɑtər‚pɑs]
magnifying glass	lupe (m/f)	['lʉpə]

measuring instrument	måleinstrument (n)	['moːlə instrʉ'mɛnt]
to measure (vt)	å måle	[ɔ 'moːlə]
scale (of thermometer, etc.)	skala (m)	['skɑlɑ]
readings	avlesninger (m/f pl)	['ɑv‚lesniŋər]

compressor	kompressor (m)	[kʊm'presʊr]
microscope	mikroskop (n)	[mikrʊ'skʊp]

pump (e.g. water ~)	pumpe (m/f)	['pʉmpə]
robot	robot (m)	['rɔbɔt]
laser	laser (m)	['lɑsər]

spanner	skrunøkkel (m)	['skrʉ‚nøkəl]
adhesive tape	pakketeip (m)	['pɑkə‚tɛjp]
glue	lim (n)	['lim]
sandpaper	sandpapir (n)	['sɑnpɑ‚pir]
spring	fjær (m/f)	['fjær]

magnet	**magnet** (m)	[maŋ'net]
gloves	**hansker** (m pl)	['hanskər]
rope	**reip, rep** (n)	['ræjp], ['rɛp]
cord	**snor** (m/f)	['snʊr]
wire (e.g. telephone ~)	**ledning** (m)	['ledniŋ]
cable	**kabel** (m)	['kabəl]
sledgehammer	**slegge** (m/f)	['ʂlegə]
prybar	**spett, jernspett** (n)	['spɛt], ['jæːn̩ˌspɛt]
ladder	**stige** (m)	['stiːə]
stepladder	**trappstige** (m/f)	['trapˌstiːə]
to screw (tighten)	**å skru fast**	[ɔ 'skrʉ 'fast]
to unscrew (lid, filter, etc.)	**å skru løs**	[ɔ 'skrʉ ˌløs]
to tighten (e.g. with a clamp)	**å klemme**	[ɔ 'klemə]
to glue, to stick	**å klistre, å lime**	[ɔ 'klistrə], [ɔ 'limə]
to cut (vt)	**å skjære**	[ɔ 'ʂæːrə]
malfunction (fault)	**funksjonsfeil** (m)	['fʉnkʂɔnsˌfæjl]
repair (mending)	**reparasjon** (m)	[reparɑ'ʂʊn]
to repair, to fix (vt)	**å reparere**	[ɔ repɑ'rerə]
to adjust (machine, etc.)	**å justere**	[ɔ jʉ'sterə]
to check (to examine)	**å sjekke**	[ɔ 'ʂɛkə]
checking	**kontroll** (m)	[kʊn'trɔl]
readings	**avlesninger** (m/f pl)	['avˌlesniŋər]
reliable, solid (machine)	**pålitelig**	[pɔ'liteli]
complex (adj)	**komplisert**	[kʊmpli'sɛːt]
to rust (get rusted)	**å ruste**	[ɔ 'rʉstə]
rusty (adj)	**rusten, rustet**	['rʉstən], ['rʉstət]
rust	**rust** (m/f)	['rʉst]

TECHNICAL EQUIPMENT. TRANSPORT

Transport

105. Aeroplane

aeroplane	fly (n)	['fly]
air ticket	flybillett (m)	['fly bi'let]
airline	flyselskap (n)	['flysel,skap]
airport	flyplass (m)	['fly,plas]
supersonic (adj)	overlyds-	['ɔvə,lyds-]
captain	kaptein (m)	[kap'tæjn]
crew	besetning (m/f)	[be'sɛtniŋ]
pilot	pilot (m)	[pi'lɔt]
stewardess	flyvertinne (m/f)	[flyvɛ:'ʈinə]
navigator	styrmann (m)	['styr,man]
wings	vinger (m pl)	['viŋər]
tail	hale (m)	['halə]
cockpit	cockpit, førerkabin (m)	['kɔkpit], ['førərka,bin]
engine	motor (m)	['mɔtʊr]
undercarriage (landing gear)	landingshjul (n)	['laniŋs,jʉl]
turbine	turbin (m)	[tʉr'bin]
propeller	propell (m)	[prʊ'pɛl]
black box	svart boks (m)	['sva:ʈ bɔks]
yoke (control column)	ratt (n)	['rat]
fuel	brensel (n)	['brɛnsəl]
safety card	sikkerhetsbrosjyre (m)	['sikərhɛts,brɔ'ʂyrə]
oxygen mask	oksygenmaske (m/f)	['ɔksygən,maskə]
uniform	uniform (m)	[ʉni'fɔrm]
lifejacket	redningsvest (m)	['rɛdniŋs,vɛst]
parachute	fallskjerm (m)	['fal,ʂærm]
takeoff	start (m)	['sta:ʈ]
to take off (vi)	å løfte	[ɔ 'lœftə]
runway	startbane (m)	['sta:ʈ,banə]
visibility	siktbarhet (m)	['siktbar,het]
flight (act of flying)	flyging (m/f)	['flygiŋ]
altitude	høyde (m)	['højdə]
air pocket	lufthull (n)	['lʉft,hʉl]
seat	plass (m)	['plas]
headphones	hodetelefoner (n pl)	['hɔdətelə,fʊnər]
folding tray (tray table)	klappbord (n)	['klap,bʊr]
airplane window	vindu (n)	['vindʉ]
aisle	midtgang (m)	['mit,gaŋ]

ﾠ‌

‌‌

106. Train

English	Norwegian	IPA
train	tog (n)	['tɔg]
commuter train	lokaltog (n)	[lɔ'kal̩tɔg]
express train	ekspresstog (n)	[ɛks'prɛs̩tɔg]
diesel locomotive	diesellokomotiv (n)	['disəl lʉkɔmɔ'tiv]
steam locomotive	damplokomotiv (n)	['damp lʉkɔmɔ'tiv]
coach, carriage	vogn (m)	['vɔŋn]
buffet car	restaurantvogn (m/f)	[rɛstʉ'raŋ̩vɔŋn]
rails	skinner (m/f pl)	['ʂinər]
railway	jernbane (m)	['jæːn̩banə]
sleeper (track support)	sville (m/f)	['svilə]
platform (railway ~)	perrong, plattform (m/f)	[pɛ'rɔŋ], ['platfɔrm]
platform (~ 1, 2, etc.)	spor (n)	['spʊr]
semaphore	semafor (m)	[sema'fʊr]
station	stasjon (m)	[sta'ʂʉn]
train driver	lokfører (m)	['lʉk̩førər]
porter (of luggage)	bærer (m)	['bærər]
carriage attendant	betjent (m)	['be'tjɛnt]
passenger	passasjer (m)	[pasa'ʂɛr]
ticket inspector	billett inspektør (m)	[bi'let inspɛk'tør]
corridor (in train)	korridor (m)	[kʉri'dɔr]
emergency brake	nødbrems (m)	['nød̩brɛms]
compartment	kupé (m)	[kʉ'pe]
berth	køye (m/f)	['køjə]
upper berth	overkøye (m/f)	['ɔvər̩køjə]
lower berth	underkøye (m/f)	['ʉnər̩køjə]
bed linen, bedding	sengetøy (n)	['sɛŋə̩tøj]
ticket	billett (m)	[bi'let]
timetable	rutetabell (m)	['rʉtə̩ta'bɛl]
information display	informasjonstavle (m/f)	[infɔrma'ʂʉns ̩tavlə]
to leave, to depart	å avgå	[ɔ 'avgɔ]
departure (of train)	avgang (m)	['av̩gaŋ]
to arrive (ab. train)	å ankomme	[ɔ 'an̩kɔmə]
arrival	ankomst (m)	['an̩kɔmst]
to arrive by train	å ankomme med toget	[ɔ 'an̩kɔmə me 'tɔgə]
to get on the train	å gå på toget	[ɔ gɔ pɔ 'tɔgə]
to get off the train	å gå av toget	[ɔ gɔ a: 'tɔgə]
train crash	togulykke (m/n)	['tɔg ʉ'lʏkə]
to derail (vi)	å spore av	[ɔ 'spʉrə a:]
steam locomotive	damplokomotiv (n)	['damp lʉkɔmɔ'tiv]
stoker, fireman	fyrbøter (m)	['fyr̩bøtər]
firebox	fyrrom (n)	['fyr̩rʊm]
coal	kull (n)	['kʉl]

107. Ship

ship	skip (n)	['ṣip]
vessel	fartøy (n)	['fɑː‚tøj]
steamship	dampskip (n)	['dɑmp‚ṣip]
riverboat	elvebåt (m)	['ɛlvə‚bot]
cruise ship	cruiseskip (n)	['krʉs‚ṣip]
cruiser	krysser (m)	['krʏsər]
yacht	jakt (m/f)	['jakt]
tugboat	bukserbåt (m)	[bʉk'ser‚bot]
barge	lastepram (m)	['lɑstə‚prɑm]
ferry	ferje, ferge (m/f)	['færjə], ['færgə]
sailing ship	seilbåt (n)	['sæjl‚bot]
brigantine	brigantin (m)	[brigɑn'tin]
ice breaker	isbryter (m)	['is‚brytər]
submarine	ubåt (m)	['ʉː‚bot]
boat (flat-bottomed ~)	båt (m)	['bot]
dinghy	jolle (m/f)	['jɔlə]
lifeboat	livbåt (m)	['liv‚bot]
motorboat	motorbåt (m)	['mɔtʉr‚bot]
captain	kaptein (m)	[kɑp'tæjn]
seaman	matros (m)	[mɑ'trʊs]
sailor	sjømann (m)	['ṣø‚mɑn]
crew	besetning (m/f)	[be'sɛtniŋ]
boatswain	båtsmann (m)	['bɔs‚mɑn]
ship's boy	skipsgutt, jungmann (m)	['ṣips‚gʉt], ['jʉŋ‚mɑn]
cook	kokk (m)	['kʊk]
ship's doctor	skipslege (m)	['ṣips‚legə]
deck	dekk (n)	['dɛk]
mast	mast (m/f)	['mɑst]
sail	seil (n)	['sæjl]
hold	lasterom (n)	['lɑstə‚rʊm]
bow (prow)	baug (m)	['bæu]
stern	akterende (m)	['ɑktə‚rɛnə]
oar	åre (m)	['oːrə]
screw propeller	propell (m)	[prʊ'pɛl]
cabin	hytte (m)	['hʏtə]
wardroom	offisersmesse (m/f)	[ɔfi'sɛrs‚mɛsə]
engine room	maskinrom (n)	[mɑ'ṣin‚rʊm]
bridge	kommandobro (m/f)	[kɔ'mɑndʉ‚brʊ]
radio room	radiorom (m)	['rɑdiʉ‚rʊm]
wave (radio)	bølge (m)	['bølgə]
logbook	loggbok (m/f)	['lɔg‚bʊk]
spyglass	langkikkert (m)	['lɑŋ‚kikeːt]
bell	klokke (m/f)	['klɔkə]

flag	flagg (n)	['flɑg]
hawser (mooring ~)	trosse (m/f)	['trʊsə]
knot (bowline, etc.)	knute (m)	['knʉtə]

| deckrails | rekkverk (n) | ['rɛk‚værk] |
| gangway | landgang (m) | ['lɑn‚gɑŋ] |

anchor	anker (n)	['ɑnkər]
to weigh anchor	å lette anker	[ɔ 'letə 'ɑnkər]
to drop anchor	å kaste anker	[ɔ 'kɑstə 'ɑnkər]
anchor chain	ankerkjetting (m)	['ɑnkər‚çɛtiŋ]

port (harbour)	havn (m/f)	['hɑvn]
quay, wharf	kai (m/f)	['kɑj]
to berth (moor)	å fortøye	[ɔ fɔːˈʈøjə]
to cast off	å kaste loss	[ɔ 'kɑstə lɔs]

trip, voyage	reise (m/f)	['ræjsə]
cruise (sea trip)	cruise (n)	['krʉs]
course (route)	kurs (m)	['kʉʂ]
route (itinerary)	rute (m/f)	['rʉtə]

fairway (safe water channel)	seilrende (m)	['sæjl‚rɛnə]
shallows	grunne (m/f)	['grʉnə]
to run aground	å gå på grunn	[ɔ 'gɔ pɔ 'grʉn]

storm	storm (m)	['stɔrm]
signal	signal (n)	[siŋ'nɑl]
to sink (vi)	å synke	[ɔ 'sʏnkə]
Man overboard!	Mann over bord!	['mɑn ‚ɔvər 'bʊr]
SOS (distress signal)	SOS (n)	[ɛsʊ'ɛs]
ring buoy	livbøye (m/f)	['liv‚bøjə]

108. Airport

airport	flyplass (m)	['fly‚plɑs]
aeroplane	fly (n)	['fly]
airline	flyselskap (n)	['flysəl‚skɑp]
air traffic controller	flygeleder (m)	['flygə‚ledər]

departure	avgang (m)	['ɑv‚gɑŋ]
arrival	ankomst (m)	['ɑn‚kɔmst]
to arrive (by plane)	å ankomme	[ɔ 'ɑn‚kɔmə]

| departure time | avgangstid (m/f) | ['ɑvgɑŋs‚tid] |
| arrival time | ankomsttid (m/f) | [ɑn'kɔms‚tid] |

| to be delayed | å bli forsinket | [ɔ 'bli fɔ'sinkət] |
| flight delay | avgangsforsinkelse (m) | ['ɑvgɑŋs fɔ'sinkəlsə] |

information board	informasjonstavle (m/f)	[infɔrmɑ'ʂʊns ‚tɑvlə]
information	informasjon (m)	[infɔrmɑ'ʂʊn]
to announce (vt)	å meddele	[ɔ 'mɛd‚delə]
flight (e.g. next ~)	fly (n)	['fly]

| customs | toll (m) | ['tɔl] |
| customs officer | tollbetjent (m) | ['tɔlbe,tjɛnt] |

customs declaration	tolldeklarasjon (m)	['tɔldɛklara'ʂʊn]
to fill in (vt)	å utfylle	[ɔ 'ʉt,fʏlə]
to fill in the declaration	å utfylle en tolldeklarasjon	[ɔ 'ʉt,fʏlə en 'tɔldɛklara,ʂʊn]
passport control	passkontroll (m)	['paskʊn,trɔl]

luggage	bagasje (m)	[ba'gaʂə]
hand luggage	håndbagasje (m)	['hɔn,ba'gaʂə]
luggage trolley	bagasjetralle (m/f)	[ba'gaʂə,tralə]

landing	landing (m)	['laniŋ]
landing strip	landingsbane (m)	['laniŋs,banə]
to land (vi)	å lande	[ɔ 'lanə]
airstairs	trapp (m/f)	['trap]

check-in	innsjekking (m/f)	['in,ʂɛkiŋ]
check-in counter	innsjekkingsskranke (m)	['in,ʂɛkiŋs ,skrankə]
to check-in (vi)	å sjekke inn	[ɔ 'ʂɛkə in]
boarding card	boardingkort (n)	['bɔ:diŋ,kɔ:t]
departure gate	gate (m/f)	['gejt]

transit	transitt (m)	[tran'sit]
to wait (vt)	å vente	[ɔ 'vɛntə]
departure lounge	ventehall (m)	['vɛntə,hal]
to see off	å ta avskjed	[ɔ 'ta 'af,ʂɛd]
to say goodbye	å si farvel	[ɔ 'si far'vɛl]

Life events

109. Holidays. Event

celebration, holiday	fest (m)	['fɛst]
national day	nasjonaldag (m)	[naʂu'nal,da]
public holiday	festdag (m)	['fɛst,da]
to commemorate (vt)	å feire	[ɔ 'fæjrə]
event (happening)	begivenhet (m/f)	[be'jiven,het]
event (organized activity)	evenement (n)	[ɛvene'maŋ]
banquet (party)	bankett (m)	[ban'kɛt]
reception (formal party)	resepsjon (m)	[resɛp'ʂun]
feast	fest (n)	['fɛst]
anniversary	årsdag (m)	['o:ʂ,da]
jubilee	jubileum (n)	[jʉbi'leʉm]
to celebrate (vt)	å feire	[ɔ 'fæjrə]
New Year	nytt år (n)	['nʏt ,o:r]
Happy New Year!	Godt nytt år!	['gɔt nʏt ,o:r]
Father Christmas	Julenissen	['jʉlə,nisən]
Christmas	Jul (m/f)	['jʉl]
Merry Christmas!	Gledelig jul!	['gledəli 'jʉl]
Christmas tree	juletre (n)	['jʉlə,trɛ]
fireworks (fireworks show)	fyrverkeri (n)	[,fyrværkə'ri]
wedding	bryllup (n)	['brʏlʉp]
groom	brudgom (m)	['brʉd,gɔm]
bride	brud (m/f)	['brʉd]
to invite (vt)	å innby, å invitere	[ɔ 'inby], [ɔ invi'terə]
invitation card	innbydelse (m)	[in'bydəlse]
guest	gjest (m)	['jɛst]
to visit (~ your parents, etc.)	å besøke	[ɔ be'søkə]
to meet the guests	å hilse på gjestene	[ɔ 'hilsə pɔ 'jɛstenə]
gift, present	gave (m/f)	['gavə]
to give (sth as present)	å gi	[ɔ 'ji]
to receive gifts	å få gaver	[ɔ 'fɔ 'gavər]
bouquet (of flowers)	bukett (m)	[bʉ'kɛt]
congratulations	lykkønskning (m/f)	['lʏk,ønskniŋ]
to congratulate (vt)	å gratulere	[ɔ gratʉ'lerə]
greetings card	gratulasjonskort (n)	[gratʉla'ʂuns,kɔ:t]
to send a postcard	å sende postkort	[ɔ 'sɛnə 'post,kɔ:t]
to get a postcard	å få postkort	[ɔ 'fɔ 'post,kɔ:t]

toast	skål (m/f)	['skɔl]
to offer (a drink, etc.)	å tilby	[ɔ 'tilby]
champagne	champagne (m)	[ʂɑm'pɑnjə]

to enjoy oneself	å more seg	[ɔ 'mʉrə sæj]
merriment (gaiety)	munterhet (m)	['mʉntər,het]
joy (emotion)	glede (m/f)	['gledə]

dance	dans (m)	['dɑns]
to dance (vi, vt)	å danse	[ɔ 'dɑnsə]

waltz	vals (m)	['vɑls]
tango	tango (m)	['tɑŋgʉ]

110. Funerals. Burial

cemetery	gravplass, kirkegård (m)	['grɑv,plɑs], ['çirkə,gɔːr]
grave, tomb	grav (m)	['grɑv]
cross	kors (n)	['kɔːʂ]
gravestone	gravstein (m)	['grɑf,stæjn]
fence	gjerde (n)	['jærə]
chapel	kapell (n)	[kɑ'pɛl]

death	død (m)	['dø]
to die (vi)	å dø	[ɔ 'dø]
the deceased	den avdøde	[den 'ɑv,dødə]
mourning	sorg (m/f)	['sɔr]

to bury (vt)	å begrave	[ɔ be'grɑvə]
undertakers	begravelsesbyrå (n)	[be'grɑvəlsəs by,ro]
funeral	begravelse (m)	[be'grɑvəlsə]

wreath	krans (m)	['krɑns]
coffin	likkiste (m/f)	['lik,çistə]
hearse	likbil (m)	['lik,bil]
shroud	likklede (n)	['lik,kledə]

funeral procession	gravfølge (n)	['grɑv,følgə]
funerary urn	askeurne (m/f)	['ɑskə,ʉːnə]
crematorium	krematorium (n)	[krɛmɑ'tʉrium]

obituary	nekrolog (m)	[nekrʉ'lɔg]
to cry (weep)	å gråte	[ɔ 'groːtə]
to sob (vi)	å hulke	[ɔ 'hʉlkə]

111. War. Soldiers

platoon	tropp (m)	['trɔp]
company	kompani (n)	[kʉmpɑ'ni]
regiment	regiment (n)	[rɛgi'mɛnt]
army	hær (m)	['hær]
division	divisjon (m)	[divi'ʂʉn]

| section, squad | tropp (m) | ['trɔp] |
| host (army) | hær (m) | ['hær] |

| soldier | soldat (m) | [sʊl'dɑt] |
| officer | offiser (m) | [ɔfi'sɛr] |

private	menig (m)	['meni]
sergeant	sersjant (m)	[sær'ʂɑnt]
lieutenant	løytnant (m)	['løjt‚nɑnt]
captain	kaptein (m)	[kɑp'tæjn]
major	major (m)	[mɑ'jɔr]
colonel	oberst (m)	['ʊbɛʂt]
general	general (m)	[gene'rɑl]

sailor	sjømann (m)	['ʂø‚mɑn]
captain	kaptein (m)	[kɑp'tæjn]
boatswain	båtsmann (m)	['bɔs‚mɑn]

artilleryman	artillerist (m)	[‚ɑːtile'rist]
paratrooper	fallskjermjeger (m)	['fɑl‚ʂærm 'jɛːgər]
pilot	flyger, flyver (m)	['flygər], ['flyvər]
navigator	styrmann (m)	['styr‚mɑn]
mechanic	mekaniker (m)	[me'kɑnikər]

pioneer (sapper)	pioner (m)	[piʊ'ner]
parachutist	fallskjermhopper (m)	['fɑl‚ʂærm 'hɔpər]
reconnaissance scout	oppklaringssoldat (m)	['ɔp‚klɑriŋ sʊl'dɑt]
sniper	skarpskytte (m)	['skɑrp‚ʂytə]
patrol (group)	patrulje (m)	[pɑ'trʉljə]
to patrol (vt)	å patruljere	[ɔ patrʉ'ljerə]
sentry, guard	vakt (m)	['vɑkt]

warrior	kriger (m)	['krigər]
hero	helt (m)	['hɛlt]
heroine	heltinne (m)	['hɛlt‚inə]
patriot	patriot (m)	[patri'ɔt]

traitor	forræder (m)	[fɔ'rædər]
to betray (vt)	å forråde	[ɔ fɔ'rɔːdə]
deserter	desertør (m)	[desæː'tør]
to desert (vi)	å desertere	[ɔ desæː'terə]

mercenary	leiesoldat (m)	['læjesʊl‚dɑt]
recruit	rekrutt (m)	[re'krʉt]
volunteer	frivillig (m)	['fri‚vili]

dead (n)	drept (m)	['drɛpt]
wounded (n)	såret (m)	['soːrə]
prisoner of war	fange (m)	['fɑŋə]

112. War. Military actions. Part 1

| war | krig (m) | ['krig] |
| to be at war | å være i krig | [ɔ 'værə i ‚krig] |

civil war	borgerkrig (m)	['bɔrgər,krig]
treacherously (adv)	lumsk, forræderisk	['lʉmsk], [fɔ'rædərisk]
declaration of war	krigserklæring (m)	['krigs ær,klæriŋ]
to declare (~ war)	å erklære	[ɔ ær'klærə]
aggression	aggresjon (m)	[agre'ʂʉn]
to attack (invade)	å angripe	[ɔ 'an,gripə]

to invade (vt)	å invadere	[ɔ invɑ'derə]
invader	angriper (m)	['an,gripər]
conqueror	erobrer (m)	[ɛ'rʉbrər]

defence	forsvar (n)	['fʉ,ʂvar]
to defend (a country, etc.)	å forsvare	[ɔ fɔ'ʂvarə]
to defend (against ...)	å forsvare seg	[ɔ fɔ'ʂvarə sæj]

enemy	fiende (m)	['fiɛndə]
foe, adversary	motstander (m)	['mʉt,stanər]
enemy (as adj)	fiendtlig	['fjɛntli]

| strategy | strategi (m) | [strate'gi] |
| tactics | taktikk (m) | [tak'tik] |

order	ordre (m)	['ɔrdrə]
command (order)	ordre, kommando (m/f)	['ɔrdrə], ['kʉ'mandʉ]
to order (vt)	å beordre	[ɔ be'ɔrdrə]
mission	oppdrag (m)	['ɔpdrag]
secret (adj)	hemmelig	['hɛməli]

battle	batalje (m)	[ba'taljə]
battle	slag (n)	['ʂlag]
combat	kamp (m)	['kamp]

attack	angrep (n)	['an,grɛp]
charge (assault)	storm (m)	['stɔrm]
to storm (vt)	å storme	[ɔ 'stɔrmə]
siege (to be under ~)	beleiring (m/f)	[be'læjriŋ]

| offensive (n) | offensiv (m), angrep (n) | ['ɔfen,sif], ['an,grɛp] |
| to go on the offensive | å angripe | [ɔ 'an,gripə] |

| retreat | retrett (m) | [rɛ'trɛt] |
| to retreat (vi) | å retirere | [ɔ reti'rerə] |

| encirclement | omringing (m/f) | ['ɔm,riŋiŋ] |
| to encircle (vt) | å omringe | [ɔ 'ɔm,riŋə] |

bombing (by aircraft)	bombing (m/f)	['bʉmbiŋ]
to drop a bomb	å slippe bombe	[ɔ 'ʂlipə 'bʉmbə]
to bomb (vt)	å bombardere	[ɔ bʉmba:'derə]
explosion	eksplosjon (m)	[ɛksplʉ'ʂʉn]

shot	skudd (n)	['skʉd]
to fire (~ a shot)	å skyte av	[ɔ 'ʂytə ɑ:]
firing (burst of ~)	skytning (m/f)	['ʂytniŋ]
to aim (to point a weapon)	å sikte på ...	[ɔ 'siktə pɔ ...]
to point (a gun)	å rette	[ɔ 'rɛtə]

to hit (the target)	å treffe	[ɔ 'trɛfə]
to sink (~ a ship)	å senke	[ɔ 'sɛnkə]
hole (in a ship)	hull (n)	['hʉl]
to founder, to sink (vi)	å synke	[ɔ 'sʏnkə]

front (war ~)	front (m)	['frɔnt]
evacuation	evakuering (m/f)	[ɛvɑkʉ'eriŋ]
to evacuate (vt)	å evakuere	[ɔ ɛvɑkʉ'erə]

trench	skyttergrav (m)	['ʂʏtə,grɑv]
barbed wire	piggtråd (m)	['pig,trɔd]
barrier (anti tank ~)	hinder (n), sperring (m/f)	['hindər], ['spɛriŋ]
watchtower	vakttårn (n)	['vɑkt,tɔːn]

military hospital	militærsykehus (n)	[mili'tær,sykə'hʉs]
to wound (vt)	å såre	[ɔ 'soːrə]
wound	sår (n)	['sor]
wounded (n)	såret (n)	['soːrə]
to be wounded	å bli såret	[ɔ 'bli 'soːrət]
serious (wound)	alvorlig	[ɑl'vɔːli]

113. War. Military actions. Part 2

captivity	fangeskap (n)	['faŋə,skap]
to take captive	å ta til fange	[ɔ 'ta til 'faŋə]
to be held captive	å være i fangeskap	[ɔ 'væːrə i 'faŋə,skap]
to be taken captive	å bli tatt til fange	[ɔ 'bli tat til 'faŋə]

concentration camp	konsentrasjonsleir (m)	[kʊnsəntra'ʂʉns,læjr]
prisoner of war	fange (m)	['faŋə]
to escape (vi)	å flykte	[ɔ 'flʏktə]

to betray (vt)	å forråde	[ɔ fɔ'rɔːdə]
betrayer	forræder (m)	[fɔ'rædər]
betrayal	forræderi (n)	[fɔrædə'ri]

| to execute (by firing squad) | å henrette ved skyting | [ɔ 'hɛn,rɛtə ve 'ʂytiŋ] |
| execution (by firing squad) | skyting (m/f) | ['ʂytiŋ] |

equipment (military gear)	mundering (m/f)	[mʉn'dɛriŋ]
shoulder board	skulderklaff (m)	['skʉldər,klɑf]
gas mask	gassmaske (m/f)	['gas,maskə]

field radio	feltradio (m)	['fɛlt,radiʊ]
cipher, code	chiffer (n)	['ʂifər]
secrecy	hemmeligholdelse (m)	['hɛməli,hɔləlsə]
password	passord (n)	['pas,uːr]

land mine	mine (m/f)	['minə]
to mine (road, etc.)	å minelegge	[ɔ 'minə,legə]
minefield	minefelt (n)	['minə,fɛlt]

| air-raid warning | flyalarm (m) | ['fly a'larm] |
| alarm (alert signal) | alarm (m) | [a'larm] |

signal	signal (n)	[siŋ'nɑl]
signal flare	signalrakett (m)	[siŋ'nɑl rɑ'kɛt]
headquarters	stab (m)	['stɑb]
reconnaissance	oppklaring (m/f)	['ɔp‚klɑriŋ]
situation	situasjon (m)	[situa'ʂʊn]
report	rapport (m)	[rɑ'pɔːt]
ambush	bakhold (n)	['bɑk‚hɔl]
reinforcement (of army)	forsterkning (m/f)	[fɔ'ʂtærkniŋ]
target	mål (n)	['mol]
training area	skytefelt (n)	['ʂytə‚fɛlt]
military exercise	manøverer (m pl)	[mɑ'nøvər]
panic	panikk (m)	[pɑ'nik]
devastation	ødeleggelse (m)	['ødə‚legəlsə]
destruction, ruins	ruiner (m pl)	[rʉ'inər]
to destroy (vt)	å ødelegge	[ɔ 'ødə‚legə]
to survive (vi, vt)	å overleve	[ɔ 'ovə‚levə]
to disarm (vt)	å avvæpne	[ɔ 'av‚væpnə]
to handle (~ a gun)	å handtere	[ɔ hɑn'terə]
Attention!	Rett! | Gi-akt!	['rɛt], ['jiː'ɑkt]
At ease!	Hvil!	['vil]
act of courage	bedrift (m)	[be'drift]
oath (vow)	ed (m)	['ɛd]
to swear (an oath)	å sverge	[ɔ 'sværgə]
decoration (medal, etc.)	belønning (m/f)	[be'lœniŋ]
to award (give medal to)	å belønne	[ɔ be'lœnə]
medal	medalje (m)	[me'daljə]
order (e.g. ~ of Merit)	orden (m)	['ɔrdən]
victory	seier (m)	['sæjər]
defeat	nederlag (n)	['nedə‚lɑg]
armistice	våpenhvile (m)	['vopən‚vilə]
standard (battle flag)	fane (m)	['fɑnə]
glory (honour, fame)	berømmelse (m)	[be'rœməlsə]
parade	parade (m)	[pɑ'rɑdə]
to march (on parade)	å marsjere	[ɔ mɑ'ʂerə]

114. Weapons

weapons	våpen (n)	['vopən]
firearms	skytevåpen (n)	['ʂytə‚vopən]
cold weapons (knives, etc.)	blankvåpen (n)	['blɑŋk‚vopən]
chemical weapons	kjemisk våpen (n)	['çemisk ‚vopən]
nuclear (adj)	kjerne-	['çæː‚ŋə-]
nuclear weapons	kjernevåpen (n)	['çæː‚ŋə‚vopən]
bomb	bombe (m)	['bʊmbə]

atomic bomb	atombombe (m)	[aˈtʊmˌbʊmbə]
pistol (gun)	pistol (m)	[piˈstʊl]
rifle	gevær (n)	[geˈvær]
submachine gun	maskinpistol (m)	[maˈʂin piˌstʊl]
machine gun	maskingevær (n)	[maˈʂin geˌvær]
muzzle	munning (m)	[ˈmʉniŋ]
barrel	løp (n)	[ˈløp]
calibre	kaliber (m/n)	[kaˈlibər]
trigger	avtrekker (m)	[ˈavˌtrɛkər]
sight (aiming device)	sikte (n)	[ˈsiktə]
magazine	magasin (n)	[magaˈsin]
butt (shoulder stock)	kolbe (m)	[ˈkɔlbə]
hand grenade	håndgranat (m)	[ˈhɔnˌgraˈnat]
explosive	sprengstoff (n)	[ˈsprɛŋˌstɔf]
bullet	kule (m/f)	[ˈkʉːlə]
cartridge	patron (m)	[paˈtrʊn]
charge	ladning (m)	[ˈladniŋ]
ammunition	ammunisjon (m)	[amʉniˈʂʊn]
bomber (aircraft)	bombefly (n)	[ˈbʊmbəˌfly]
fighter	jagerfly (n)	[ˈjagərˌfly]
helicopter	helikopter (n)	[heliˈkɔptər]
anti-aircraft gun	luftvernkanon (m)	[ˈlʉftvɛːn kaˈnʊn]
tank	stridsvogn (m/f)	[ˈstridsˌvɔŋn]
tank gun	kanon (m)	[kaˈnʊn]
artillery	artilleri (n)	[ˌaːʈileˈri]
gun (cannon, howitzer)	kanon (m)	[kaˈnʊn]
to lay (a gun)	å rette	[ɔ ˈrɛtə]
shell (projectile)	projektil (m)	[prʊekˈtil]
mortar bomb	granat (m/f)	[graˈnat]
mortar	granatkaster (m)	[graˈnatˌkastər]
splinter (shell fragment)	splint (m)	[ˈsplint]
submarine	ubåt (m)	[ˈʉːˌbot]
torpedo	torpedo (m)	[tʊrˈpedʊ]
missile	rakett (m)	[raˈkɛt]
to load (gun)	å lade	[ɔ ˈladə]
to shoot (vi)	å skyte	[ɔ ˈʂytə]
to point at (the cannon)	å sikte på ...	[ɔ ˈsiktə pɔ ...]
bayonet	bajonett (m)	[bajoˈnɛt]
rapier	kårde (m)	[ˈkoːrdə]
sabre (e.g. cavalry ~)	sabel (m)	[ˈsabəl]
spear (weapon)	spyd (n)	[ˈspyd]
bow	bue (m)	[ˈbʉːə]
arrow	pil (m/f)	[ˈpil]
musket	muskett (m)	[mʉˈskɛt]
crossbow	armbrøst (m)	[ˈarmˌbrøst]

115. Ancient people

primitive (prehistoric)	ur-	['ʉr-]
prehistoric (adj)	forhistorisk	['fɔrhiˌstʉrisk]
ancient (~ civilization)	oldtidens, antikkens	['ɔlˌtidəns], [an'tikəns]
Stone Age	Steinalderen	['stæjnˌalderən]
Bronze Age	bronsealder (m)	['brɔnsəˌaldər]
Ice Age	istid (m/f)	['isˌtid]
tribe	stamme (m)	['stɑmə]
cannibal	kannibal (m)	[kani'bɑl]
hunter	jeger (m)	['jɛ:gər]
to hunt (vi, vt)	å jage	[ɔ 'jagə]
mammoth	mammut (m)	['mɑmʉt]
cave	grotte (m/f)	['grɔtə]
fire	ild (m)	['il]
campfire	bål (n)	['bɔl]
cave painting	helleristning (m/f)	['hɛləˌristniŋ]
tool (e.g. stone axe)	redskap (m/n)	['rɛdˌskɑp]
spear	spyd (n)	['spyd]
stone axe	steinøks (m/f)	['stæjnˌøks]
to be at war	å være i krig	[ɔ 'værə i ˌkrig]
to domesticate (vt)	å temme	[ɔ 'tɛmə]
idol	idol (n)	[i'dʉl]
to worship (vt)	å dyrke	[ɔ 'dyrkə]
superstition	overtro (m)	['ɔvəˌtrʉ]
rite	ritual (n)	[ritʉ'al]
evolution	evolusjon (m)	[ɛvɔlʉ'sʉn]
development	utvikling (m/f)	['ʉtˌvikliŋ]
disappearance (extinction)	forsvinning (m/f)	[fɔ'sviniŋ]
to adapt oneself	å tilpasse seg	[ɔ 'tilˌpasə sæj]
archaeology	arkeologi (m)	[ˌɑrkeʉlʉ'gi]
archaeologist	arkeolog (m)	[ˌɑrkeʉ'lɔg]
archaeological (adj)	arkeologisk	[ˌɑrkeʉ'lɔgisk]
excavation site	utgravingssted (n)	['ʉtˌgraviŋs ˌsted]
excavations	utgravinger (m/f pl)	['ʉtˌgraviŋər]
find (object)	funn (n)	['fʉn]
fragment	fragment (n)	[frɑg'mɛnt]

116. Middle Ages

people (ethnic group)	folk (n)	['fɔlk]
peoples	folk (n pl)	['fɔlk]
tribe	stamme (m)	['stɑmə]
tribes	stammer (m pl)	['stɑmər]
barbarians	barbarer (m pl)	[bar'barər]

Gauls	gallere (m pl)	['galere]
Goths	gotere (m pl)	['gɔterə]
Slavs	slavere (m pl)	['slavɛrə]
Vikings	vikinger (m pl)	['vikiŋər]

| Romans | romere (m pl) | ['rʊmerə] |
| Roman (adj) | romersk | ['rʊmæṣk] |

Byzantines	bysantiner (m pl)	[bysan'tinər]
Byzantium	Bysants	[by'sants]
Byzantine (adj)	bysantinsk	[bysan'tinsk]

emperor	keiser (m)	['kæjsər]
leader, chief (tribal ~)	høvding (m)	['høvdiŋ]
powerful (~ king)	mektig	['mɛkti]
king	konge (m)	['kʊŋə]
ruler (sovereign)	hersker (m)	['hæṣkər]

knight	ridder (m)	['ridər]
feudal lord	føydalherre (m)	['føjdal‚hɛrə]
feudal (adj)	føydal	['føjdal]
vassal	vasall (m)	[va'sal]

duke	hertug (m)	['hæːʈʉg]
earl	greve (m)	['grevə]
baron	baron (m)	[ba'rʊn]
bishop	biskop (m)	['biskɔp]

armour	rustning (m/f)	['rʉstniŋ]
shield	skjold (n)	['ṣɔl]
sword	sverd (n)	['sværd]
visor	visir (n)	[vi'sir]
chainmail	ringbrynje (m/f)	['riŋ‚brynje]

| Crusade | korstog (n) | ['kɔːṣ‚tɔg] |
| crusader | korsfarer (m) | ['kɔːṣ‚farər] |

territory	territorium (n)	[tɛri'tʊrium]
to attack (invade)	å angripe	[ɔ 'an‚gripə]
to conquer (vt)	å erobre	[ɔ ɛ'rʊbrə]
to occupy (invade)	å okkupere	[ɔ ɔkʉ'perə]

siege (to be under ~)	beleiring (m/f)	[be'læjriŋ]
besieged (adj)	beleiret	[be'læjrət]
to besiege (vt)	å beleire	[ɔ be'læjre]

inquisition	inkvisisjon (m)	[inkvisi'ṣʊn]
inquisitor	inkvisitor (m)	[inkvi'sitʊr]
torture	tortur (m)	[tɔ:'ʈʉr]
cruel (adj)	brutal	[brʉ'tal]
heretic	kjetter (m)	['çɛtər]
heresy	kjetteri (n)	[çɛtə'ri]

seafaring	sjøfart (m)	['ṣø‚faːʈ]
pirate	pirat, sjørøver (m)	['pi'rat], ['ṣø‚røvər]
piracy	sjørøveri (n)	['ṣø røvɛ'ri]

113

boarding (attack)	entring (m/f)	['ɛntriŋ]
loot, booty	bytte (n)	['bʏtə]
treasures	skatter (m pl)	['skatər]

discovery	oppdagelse (m)	['ɔp,dagəlsə]
to discover (new land, etc.)	å oppdage	[ɔ 'ɔp,dagə]
expedition	ekspedisjon (m)	[ɛkspedi'ʂʊn]

musketeer	musketer (m)	[mʉskə'ter]
cardinal	kardinal (m)	[kɑːɖi'nɑl]
heraldry	heraldikk (m)	[herɑl'dik]
heraldic (adj)	heraldisk	[he'rɑldisk]

117. Leader. Chief. Authorities

king	konge (m)	['kʊŋə]
queen	dronning (m/f)	['drɔniŋ]
royal (adj)	kongelig	['kʊŋəli]
kingdom	kongerike (n)	['kʊŋə,rikə]

| prince | prins (m) | ['prins] |
| princess | prinsesse (m/f) | [prin'sɛsə] |

president	president (m)	[prɛsi'dɛnt]
vice-president	visepresident (m)	['visə prɛsi'dɛnt]
senator	senator (m)	[se'nɑtʊr]

monarch	monark (m)	[mʊ'nɑrk]
ruler (sovereign)	hersker (m)	['hæʂkər]
dictator	diktator (m)	[dik'tatʊr]
tyrant	tyrann (m)	[ty'rɑn]
magnate	magnat (m)	[mɑŋ'nɑt]

director	direktør (m)	[dirɛk'tør]
chief	sjef (m)	['ʂɛf]
manager (director)	forstander (m)	[fɔ'ʂtandər]
boss	boss (m)	['bɔs]
owner	eier (m)	['æjər]

leader	leder (m)	['ledər]
head (~ of delegation)	leder (m)	['ledər]
authorities	myndigheter (m pl)	['mʏndi,hetər]
superiors	overordnede (pl)	['ɔvər,ɔrdnedə]

governor	guvernør (m)	[gʉver'nør]
consul	konsul (m)	['kʊn,sʉl]
diplomat	diplomat (m)	[diplʉ'mɑt]
mayor	borgermester (m)	[bɔrgər'mɛstər]
sheriff	sheriff (m)	[ʂɛ'rif]

emperor	keiser (m)	['kæjsər]
tsar, czar	tsar (m)	['tsɑr]
pharaoh	farao (m)	['fɑrɑu]
khan	khan (m)	['kɑn]

118. Breaking the law. Criminals. Part 1

bandit	bandit (m)	[bɑn'dit]
crime	forbrytelse (m)	[fɔr'brytəlsə]
criminal (person)	forbryter (m)	[fɔr'brytər]
thief	tyv (m)	['tyv]
to steal (vi, vt)	å stjele	[ɔ 'stjelə]
to kidnap (vt)	å kidnappe	[ɔ 'kidˌnɛpə]
kidnapping	kidnapping (m)	['kidˌnɛpiŋ]
kidnapper	kidnapper (m)	['kidˌnɛpər]
ransom	løsepenger (m pl)	['løsəˌpɛŋər]
to demand ransom	å kreve løsepenger	[ɔ 'krevə 'løsəˌpɛŋər]
to rob (vt)	å rane	[ɔ 'rɑnə]
robbery	ran (n)	['rɑn]
robber	raner (m)	['rɑnər]
to extort (vt)	å presse ut	[ɔ 'prɛsə ʉt]
extortionist	utpresser (m)	['ʉtˌprɛsər]
extortion	utpressing (m/f)	['ʉtˌprɛsiŋ]
to murder, to kill	å myrde	[ɔ 'myːdə]
murder	mord (n)	['mʊr]
murderer	morder (m)	['mʊrdər]
gunshot	skudd (n)	['skʉd]
to fire (~ a shot)	å skyte av	[ɔ 'ʂytə ɑː]
to shoot to death	å skyte ned	[ɔ 'ʂytə ne]
to shoot (vi)	å skyte	[ɔ 'ʂytə]
shooting	skyting, skytning (m/f)	['ʂytiŋ], ['ʂytniŋ]
incident (fight, etc.)	hendelse (m)	['hɛndəlsə]
fight, brawl	slagsmål (n)	['ʂlɑksˌmol]
Help!	Hjelp!	['jɛlp]
victim	offer (n)	['ɔfər]
to damage (vt)	å skade	[ɔ 'skɑdə]
damage	skade (m)	['skɑdə]
dead body, corpse	lik (n)	['lik]
grave (~ crime)	alvorlig	[ɑl'vɔːli]
to attack (vt)	å anfalle	[ɔ 'ɑnˌfɑlə]
to beat (to hit)	å slå	[ɔ 'ʂlɔ]
to beat up	å klå opp	[ɔ 'klɔ ɔp]
to take (rob of sth)	å berøve	[ɔ be'røvə]
to stab to death	å stikke i hjel	[ɔ 'stikə i 'jel]
to maim (vt)	å lemleste	[ɔ 'lemˌlestə]
to wound (vt)	å såre	[ɔ 'soːrə]
blackmail	utpressing (m/f)	['ʉtˌprɛsiŋ]
to blackmail (vt)	å utpresse	[ɔ 'ʉtˌprɛsə]
blackmailer	utpresser (m)	['ʉtˌprɛsər]

protection racket	utpressing (m/f)	['ʉtˌprɛsiŋ]
racketeer	utpresser (m)	['ʉtˌprɛsər]
gangster	gangster (m)	['gɛŋstər]
mafia	mafia (m)	['mɑfiɑ]

pickpocket	lommetyv (m)	['lʊməˌtyv]
burglar	innbruddstyv (m)	['inbrʉdsˌtyv]
smuggling	smugling (m/f)	['smʉgliŋ]
smuggler	smugler (m)	['smʉglər]

forgery	forfalskning (m/f)	[fɔr'fɑlskniŋ]
to forge (counterfeit)	å forfalske	[ɔ fɔr'fɑlskə]
fake (forged)	falsk	['fɑlsk]

119. Breaking the law. Criminals. Part 2

rape	voldtekt (m)	['vɔlˌtɛkt]
to rape (vt)	å voldta	[ɔ 'vɔlˌtɑ]
rapist	voldtektsmann (m)	['vɔlˌtɛkts mɑn]
maniac	maniker (m)	['mɑnikər]

prostitute (fem.)	prostituert (m)	[prʊstitʉ'eːt]
prostitution	prostitusjon (m)	[prʊstitʉ'ʂʊn]
pimp	hallik (m)	['hɑlik]

| drug addict | narkoman (m) | [nɑrkʊ'mɑn] |
| drug dealer | narkolanger (m) | ['nɑrkɔˌlɑŋər] |

to blow up (bomb)	å sprenge	[ɔ 'sprɛŋə]
explosion	eksplosjon (m)	[ɛksplʊ'ʂʊn]
to set fire	å sette fyr	[ɔ 'sɛtə ˌfyr]
arsonist	brannstifter (m)	['brɑnˌstiftər]

terrorism	terrorisme (m)	[tɛrʊ'rismə]
terrorist	terrorist (m)	[tɛrʊ'rist]
hostage	gissel (m)	['jisəl]

to swindle (deceive)	å bedra	[ɔ be'drɑ]
swindle, deception	bedrag (n)	[be'drɑg]
swindler	bedrager, svindler (m)	[be'drɑgər], ['svindlər]

to bribe (vt)	å bestikke	[ɔ be'stikə]
bribery	bestikkelse (m)	[be'stikəlsə]
bribe	bestikkelse (m)	[be'stikəlsə]

poison	gift (m/f)	['jift]
to poison (vt)	å forgifte	[ɔ fɔr'jiftə]
to poison oneself	å forgifte seg selv	[ɔ fɔr'jiftə sæj sɛl]

| suicide (act) | selvmord (n) | ['sɛlˌmʊr] |
| suicide (person) | selvmorder (m) | ['sɛlˌmʊrdər] |

| to threaten (vt) | å true | [ɔ 'trʉə] |
| threat | trussel (m) | ['trʉsəl] |

| to make an attempt | å begå mordforsøk | [ɔ be'gɔ 'mʊrdfɔˌsøk] |
| attempt (attack) | mordforsøk (n) | ['mʊrdfɔˌsøk] |

| to steal (a car) | å stjele | [ɔ 'stjelə] |
| to hijack (a plane) | å kapre | [ɔ 'kaprə] |

| revenge | hevn (m) | ['hɛvn] |
| to avenge (get revenge) | å hevne | [ɔ 'hɛvnə] |

to torture (vt)	å torturere	[ɔ tɔ:ʈu'rerə]
torture	tortur (m)	[tɔ:'ʈur]
to torment (vt)	å plage	[ɔ 'plagə]

pirate	pirat, sjørøver (m)	['pi'rat], ['ʂøˌrøvər]
hooligan	bølle (m)	['bølə]
armed (adj)	bevæpnet	[be'væpnət]
violence	vold (m)	['vɔl]
illegal (unlawful)	illegal	['ileˌgal]

| spying (espionage) | spionasje (m) | [spiʊ'naʂə] |
| to spy (vi) | å spionere | [ɔ spiʊ'nerə] |

120. Police. Law. Part 1

| justice | justis (m), rettspleie (m/f) | ['jʉ'stis], ['rɛtsˌplæje] |
| court (see you in ~) | rettssal (m) | ['rɛtsˌsal] |

judge	dommer (m)	['dɔmər]
jurors	lagrettemedlemmer (n pl)	['lagˌrɛtə medle'mer]
jury trial	lagrette, juryordning (m)	['lagˌrɛtə], ['jʉriˌɔrdniŋ]
to judge (vt)	å dømme	[ɔ 'dœmə]

lawyer, barrister	advokat (m)	[advʊ'kat]
defendant	anklaget (m)	['anˌklaget]
dock	anklagebenk (m)	[an'klagəˌbɛnk]

| charge | anklage (m) | ['anˌklagə] |
| accused | anklagede (m) | ['anˌklagedə] |

| sentence | dom (m) | ['dɔm] |
| to sentence (vt) | å dømme | [ɔ 'dœmə] |

guilty (culprit)	skyldige (m)	['ʂyldiə]
to punish (vt)	å straffe	[ɔ 'strafə]
punishment	straff, avstraffelse (m)	['straf], ['afˌstrafəlsə]

fine (penalty)	bot (m/f)	['bʊt]
life imprisonment	livsvarig fengsel (n)	['lifsˌvari 'fɛŋsəl]
death penalty	dødsstraff (m/f)	['dødˌstraf]
electric chair	elektrisk stol (m)	[ɛ'lektrisk ˌstʊl]
gallows	galge (m)	['galgə]

| to execute (vt) | å henrette | [ɔ 'hɛnˌrɛtə] |
| execution | henrettelse (m) | ['hɛnˌrɛtəlsə] |

| prison | fengsel (n) | ['fɛŋsəl] |
| cell | celle (m) | ['sɛlə] |

escort	eskorte (m)	[ɛs'kɔːṭə]
prison officer	fangevokter (m)	['faŋə‚vɔktər]
prisoner	fange (m)	['faŋə]

| handcuffs | håndjern (n pl) | ['hɔnˌjæːn̩] |
| to handcuff (vt) | å sette håndjern | [ɔ 'sɛtə 'hɔnˌjæːn̩] |

prison break	flykt (m/f)	['flʏkt]
to break out (vi)	å flykte, å rømme	[ɔ 'flʏktə], [ɔ 'rœmə]
to disappear (vi)	å forsvinne	[ɔ fɔ'ʂvinə]
to release (from prison)	å løslate	[ɔ 'løsˌlatə]
amnesty	amnesti (m)	[ɑmnɛ'sti]

police	politi (n)	[pʊli'ti]
police officer	politi (m)	[pʊli'ti]
police station	politistasjon (m)	[pʊli'tiˌsta'ʂʊn]
truncheon	gummikølle (m/f)	['gʉmiˌkølə]
megaphone (loudhailer)	megafon (m)	[mega'fʉn]

patrol car	patruljebil (m)	[pɑ'trʉljəˌbil]
siren	sirene (m/f)	[si'renə]
to turn on the siren	å slå på sirenen	[ɔ 'ʂlɔ pɔ si'renən]
siren call	sirene hyl (n)	[si'renə ˌhyl]

crime scene	åsted (n)	['ɔsted]
witness	vitne (n)	['vitnə]
freedom	frihet (m)	['friˌhet]
accomplice	medskyldig (m)	['mɛˌsyldi]
to flee (vi)	å flykte	[ɔ 'flʏktə]
trace (to leave a ~)	spor (n)	['spʊr]

121. Police. Law. Part 2

search (investigation)	ettersøking (m/f)	['ɛtəˌsøkiŋ]
to look for ...	å søke etter ...	[ɔ 'søkə ˌɛtər ...]
suspicion	mistanke (m)	['misˌtankə]
suspicious (e.g., ~ vehicle)	mistenkelig	[mis'tɛnkəli]
to stop (cause to halt)	å stoppe	[ɔ 'stɔpə]
to detain (keep in custody)	å anholde	[ɔ 'anˌhɔlə]

case (lawsuit)	sak (m/f)	['sɑk]
investigation	etterforskning (m/f)	['ɛtərˌfɔʂkniŋ]
detective	detektiv (m)	[detɛk'tiv]
investigator	etterforsker (m)	['ɛtərˌfɔʂkər]
hypothesis	versjon (m)	[væ'ʂʊn]

motive	motiv (n)	[mʊ'tiv]
interrogation	forhør (n)	[fɔr'hør]
to interrogate (vt)	å forhøre	[ɔ fɔr'hørə]
to question (~ neighbors, etc.)	å avhøre	[ɔ 'avˌhørə]

check (identity ~)	**sjekking** (m/f)	['ʂɛkiŋ]
round-up	**rassia, razzia** (m)	['rɑsiɑ]
search (~ warrant)	**ransakelse** (m)	['rɑnˌsɑkəlsə]
chase (pursuit)	**jakt** (m/f)	['jakt]
to pursue, to chase	**å forfølge**	[ɔ fɔr'følə]
to track (a criminal)	**å spore**	[ɔ 'spʊrə]
arrest	**arrest** (m)	[ɑ'rɛst]
to arrest (sb)	**å arrestere**	[ɔ ɑrɛ'sterə]
to catch (thief, etc.)	**å fange**	[ɔ 'fɑŋə]
capture	**pågripelse** (m)	['pɔˌgripəlsə]
document	**dokument** (n)	[dɔkʉ'mɛnt]
proof (evidence)	**bevis** (n)	[be'vis]
to prove (vt)	**å bevise**	[ɔ be'visə]
footprint	**fotspor** (n)	['fʊtˌspʊr]
fingerprints	**fingeravtrykk** (n pl)	['fiŋərˌɑvtrʏk]
piece of evidence	**bevis** (n)	[be'vis]
alibi	**alibi** (n)	['ɑlibi]
innocent (not guilty)	**uskyldig**	[ʉ'ʂyldi]
injustice	**urettferdighet** (m)	['ʉrɛtfærdiˌhet]
unjust, unfair (adj)	**urettferdig**	['ʉrɛtˌfærdi]
criminal (adj)	**kriminell**	[krimi'nɛl]
to confiscate (vt)	**å konfiskere**	[ɔ kʊnfi'skerə]
drug (illegal substance)	**narkotika** (m)	[nɑr'kɔtikɑ]
weapon, gun	**våpen** (n)	['vɔpən]
to disarm (vt)	**å avvæpne**	[ɔ 'ɑvˌvæpnə]
to order (command)	**å befale**	[ɔ be'fɑlə]
to disappear (vi)	**å forsvinne**	[ɔ fɔ'ʂvinə]
law	**lov** (m)	['lɔv]
legal, lawful (adj)	**lovlig**	['lɔvli]
illegal, illicit (adj)	**ulovlig**	[ʉ'lɔvli]
responsibility (blame)	**ansvar** (n)	['ɑnˌsvɑr]
responsible (adj)	**ansvarlig**	[ɑns'vɑ:ɭi]

NATURE

The Earth. Part 1

122. Outer space

space	rommet, kosmos (n)	['rʊmə], ['kɔsmɔs]
space (as adj)	rom-	['rʊm-]
outer space	ytre rom (n)	['ytrə ˌrʊm]
world	verden (m)	['værdən]
universe	univers (n)	[ʉni'væs̪]
galaxy	galakse (m)	[gɑ'lɑksə]
star	stjerne (m/f)	['stjæːŋə]
constellation	stjernebilde (n)	['stjæːŋəˌbildə]
planet	planet (m)	[plɑ'net]
satellite	satellitt (m)	[sɑtɛ'lit]
meteorite	meteoritt (m)	[meteʊ'rit]
comet	komet (m)	[kʊ'met]
asteroid	asteroide (n)	[ɑsterʊ'idə]
orbit	bane (m)	['bɑnə]
to revolve	å rotere	[ɔ rɔ'terə]
(~ around the Earth)		
atmosphere	atmosfære (m)	[ɑtmʊ'sfærə]
the Sun	Solen	['sʊlən]
solar system	solsystem (n)	['sʊl sʏ'stem]
solar eclipse	solformørkelse (m)	['sʊl fɔr'mœrkəlsə]
the Earth	Jorden	['juːrən]
the Moon	Månen	['moːnən]
Mars	Mars	['mɑʂ]
Venus	Venus	['venʉs]
Jupiter	Jupiter	['jʉpitər]
Saturn	Saturn	['sɑˌtʉːn]
Mercury	Merkur	[mær'kʉr]
Uranus	Uranus	[ʉ'rɑnʉs]
Neptune	Neptun	[nɛp'tʉn]
Pluto	Pluto	['plʉtʊ]
Milky Way	Melkeveien	['mɛlkəˌvæjən]
Great Bear (Ursa Major)	den Store Bjørn	['dən 'stʉrə ˌbjœːn]
North Star	Nordstjernen, Polaris	['nuːrˌstjæːŋən], [pɔ'laris]
Martian	marsbeboer (m)	['mɑʂˌbebʊər]
extraterrestrial (n)	utenomjordisk vesen (n)	['ʉtənɔmˌjuːrdisk 'vesən]

| alien | romvesen (n) | ['rʊm‚vesən] |
| flying saucer | flygende tallerken (m) | ['flygenə ta'lærkən] |

spaceship	romskip (n)	['rʊm‚ʃip]
space station	romstasjon (m)	['rʊm‚sta'ʂʊn]
blast-off	start (m), oppskyting (m/f)	['sta:t], ['ɔp‚ʂytiŋ]

engine	motor (m)	['mɔtʊr]
nozzle	dyse (m)	['dysə]
fuel	brensel (n), drivstoff (n)	['brɛnsəl], ['drif‚stɔf]

cockpit, flight deck	cockpit (m), flydekk (n)	['kɔkpit], ['fly‚dɛk]
aerial	antenne (m)	[an'tɛnə]
porthole	koøye (n)	['kʊ‚øjə]
solar panel	solbatteri (n)	['sʊl batɛ'ri]
spacesuit	romdrakt (m/f)	['rʊm‚drakt]

| weightlessness | vektløshet (m/f) | ['vɛktløs‚het] |
| oxygen | oksygen (n) | ['ɔksy'gen] |

| docking (in space) | dokking (m/f) | ['dɔkiŋ] |
| to dock (vi, vt) | å dokke | [ɔ 'dɔkə] |

observatory	observatorium (n)	[ɔbsərva'tʊrium]
telescope	teleskop (n)	[tele'skʊp]
to observe (vt)	å observere	[ɔ ɔbsɛr'verə]
to explore (vt)	å utforske	[ɔ 'ʉt‚fɔʂkə]

123. The Earth

the Earth	Jorden	['ju:rən]
the globe (the Earth)	jordklode (m)	['ju:r‚klɔdə]
planet	planet (m)	[pla'net]

atmosphere	atmosfære (m)	[atmʊ'sfærə]
geography	geografi (m)	[geʊgra'fi]
nature	natur (m)	[na'tʉr]

globe (table ~)	globus (m)	['glɔbʉs]
map	kart (n)	['ka:t]
atlas	atlas (n)	['atlas]

| Europe | Europa | [ɛʉ'rʊpa] |
| Asia | Asia | ['asia] |

| Africa | Afrika | ['afrika] |
| Australia | Australia | [aʉ'stralia] |

America	Amerika	[a'merika]
North America	Nord-Amerika	['nʊ:r a'merika]
South America	Sør-Amerika	['sør a'merika]

| Antarctica | Antarktis | [an'tarktis] |
| the Arctic | Arktis | ['arktis] |

124. Cardinal directions

north	nord (n)	['nuːr]
to the north	mot nord	[mʊt 'nuːr]
in the north	i nord	[i 'nuːr]
northern (adj)	nordlig	['nuːrli]
south	syd, sør	['syd], ['sør]
to the south	mot sør	[mʊt 'sør]
in the south	i sør	[i 'sør]
southern (adj)	sydlig, sørlig	['sydli], ['søːɭi]
west	vest (m)	['vɛst]
to the west	mot vest	[mʊt 'vɛst]
in the west	i vest	[i 'vɛst]
western (adj)	vestlig, vest-	['vɛstli]
east	øst (m)	['øst]
to the east	mot øst	[mʊt 'øst]
in the east	i øst	[i 'øst]
eastern (adj)	østlig	['østli]

125. Sea. Ocean

sea	hav (n)	['hɑv]
ocean	verdenshav (n)	[værdəns'hɑv]
gulf (bay)	bukt (m/f)	['bʉkt]
straits	sund (n)	['sʉn]
land (solid ground)	fastland (n)	['fɑst‚lɑn]
continent (mainland)	fastland, kontinent (n)	['fɑst‚lɑn], [kʊnti'nɛnt]
island	øy (m/f)	['øj]
peninsula	halvøy (m/f)	['hɑl‚øːj]
archipelago	skjærgård (m), arkipelag (n)	['ʂær‚gɔr], [ɑrkipe'lɑg]
bay, cove	bukt (m/f)	['bʉkt]
harbour	havn (m/f)	['hɑvn]
lagoon	lagune (m)	[lɑ'gʉnə]
cape	nes (n), kapp (n)	['nes], ['kɑp]
atoll	atoll (m)	[ɑ'tɔl]
reef	rev (n)	['rev]
coral	korall (m)	[kʊ'rɑl]
coral reef	korallrev (n)	[kʊ'rɑl‚rɛv]
deep (adj)	dyp	['dyp]
depth (deep water)	dybde (m)	['dʏbdə]
abyss	avgrunn (m)	['ɑv‚grʉn]
trench (e.g. Mariana ~)	dyphavsgrop (m/f)	['dyphɑfs‚grɔp]
current (Ocean ~)	strøm (m)	['strøm]
to surround (bathe)	å omgi	[ɔ 'ɔmˌji]
shore	kyst (m)	['çyst]

coast	kyst (m)	['çyst]
flow (flood tide)	flo (m/f)	['flʊ]
ebb (ebb tide)	ebbe (m), fjære (m/f)	['ɛbə], ['fjærə]
shoal	sandbanke (m)	['san,bankə]
bottom (~ of the sea)	bunn (m)	['bʉn]

wave	bølge (m)	['bølgə]
crest (~ of a wave)	bølgekam (m)	['bølgə,kam]
spume (sea foam)	skum (n)	['skʉm]

storm (sea storm)	storm (m)	['stɔrm]
hurricane	orkan (m)	[ɔr'kan]
tsunami	tsunami (m)	[tsʉ'nami]
calm (dead ~)	stille (m/f)	['stilə]
quiet, calm (adj)	stille	['stilə]

| pole | pol (m) | ['pʊl] |
| polar (adj) | pol-, polar | ['pʊl-], [pʊ'lar] |

latitude	bredde, latitude (m)	['brɛdə], ['lati,tʉdə]
longitude	lengde (m/f)	['leŋdə]
parallel	breddegrad (m)	['brɛdə,grad]
equator	ekvator (m)	[ɛ'kvatʊr]

sky	himmel (m)	['himəl]
horizon	horisont (m)	[hʊri'sɔnt]
air	luft (f)	['lʉft]

lighthouse	fyr (n)	['fyr]
to dive (vi)	å dykke	[ɔ 'dʏkə]
to sink (ab. boat)	å synke	[ɔ 'sʏnkə]
treasures	skatter (m pl)	['skatər]

126. Seas & Oceans names

Atlantic Ocean	Atlanterhavet	[at'lantər,have]
Indian Ocean	Indiahavet	['india,have]
Pacific Ocean	Stillehavet	['stilə,have]
Arctic Ocean	Polhavet	['pol,have]

Black Sea	Svartehavet	['sva:ʈə,have]
Red Sea	Rødehavet	['rødə,have]
Yellow Sea	Gulehavet	['gʉlə,have]
White Sea	Kvitsjøen, Hvitehavet	['kvit,sø:n], ['vit,have]

Caspian Sea	Kaspihavet	['kaspi,have]
Dead Sea	Dødehavet	['dødə'have]
Mediterranean Sea	Middelhavet	['midəl,have]

| Aegean Sea | Egeerhavet | [ɛ'ge:ər,have] |
| Adriatic Sea | Adriahavet | ['adria,have] |

| Arabian Sea | Arabiahavet | [a'rabia,have] |
| Sea of Japan | Japanhavet | ['japan,have] |

| Bering Sea | Beringhavet | ['berɪŋ,hɑve] |
| South China Sea | Sør-Kina-havet | ['sør,çinɑ 'hɑve] |

Coral Sea	Korallhavet	[kʊ'rɑl,hɑve]
Tasman Sea	Tasmanhavet	[tɑs'mɑn,hɑve]
Caribbean Sea	Karibhavet	[kɑ'rib,hɑve]

| Barents Sea | Barentshavet | ['bɑrɛns,hɑve] |
| Kara Sea | Karahavet | ['kɑrɑ,hɑve] |

North Sea	Nordsjøen	['nuːr,ʂøːn]
Baltic Sea	Østersjøen	['østə,ʂøːn]
Norwegian Sea	Norskehavet	['nɔʂkə,hɑve]

127. Mountains

mountain	fjell (n)	['fjɛl]
mountain range	fjellkjede (m)	['fjɛl,çɛːdə]
mountain ridge	fjellrygg (m)	['fjɛl,rʏg]

summit, top	topp (m)	['tɔp]
peak	tind (m)	['tin]
foot (~ of the mountain)	fot (m)	['fʊt]
slope (mountainside)	skråning (m)	['skrɔnɪŋ]

volcano	vulkan (m)	[vʉl'kɑn]
active volcano	virksom vulkan (m)	['virksɔm vʉl'kɑn]
dormant volcano	utslukt vulkan (m)	['ʉt,slʉkt vʉl'kɑn]

eruption	utbrudd (n)	['ʉt,brʉd]
crater	krater (n)	['krɑtər]
magma	magma (m/n)	['mɑgmɑ]
lava	lava (m)	['lɑvɑ]
molten (~ lava)	glødende	['glødenə]

canyon	canyon (m)	['kɑnjən]
gorge	gjel (n), kløft (m)	['jel], ['klœft]
crevice	renne (m/f)	['rɛnə]
abyss (chasm)	avgrunn (m)	['ɑv,grʉn]

pass, col	pass (n)	['pɑs]
plateau	platå (n)	[plɑ'to]
cliff	klippe (m)	['klipə]
hill	ås (m)	['ɔs]

glacier	bre, jøkel (m)	['bre], ['jøkəl]
waterfall	foss (m)	['fɔs]
geyser	geysir (m)	['gɛjsir]
lake	innsjø (m)	['in'ʂø]

plain	slette (m/f)	['ʂletə]
landscape	landskap (n)	['lɑn,skɑp]
echo	ekko (n)	['ɛkʊ]
alpinist	alpinist (m)	[ɑlpi'nist]

rock climber	fjellklatrer (m)	['fjɛlˌklɑtrər]
to conquer (in climbing)	å erobre	[ɔ ɛ'rʊbrə]
climb (an easy ~)	bestigning (m/f)	[be'stigniŋ]

128. Mountains names

The Alps	Alpene	['ɑlpenə]
Mont Blanc	Mont Blanc	[ˌmɔn'blɑn]
The Pyrenees	Pyreneene	[pyre'ne:ənə]

The Carpathians	Karpatene	[kɑr'pɑtenə]
The Ural Mountains	Uralfjellene	[ʉ'rɑl ˌfjɛlenə]
The Caucasus Mountains	Kaukasus	['kɑʉkɑsʉs]
Mount Elbrus	Elbrus	[ɛl'brʉs]

The Altai Mountains	Altaj	[ɑl'tɑj]
The Tian Shan	Tien Shan	[ti'enˌʂɑn]
The Pamir Mountains	Pamir	[pɑ'mir]
The Himalayas	Himalaya	[himɑ'lɑjɑ]
Mount Everest	Everest	['ɛve'rɛst]

| The Andes | Andes | ['ɑndəs] |
| Mount Kilimanjaro | Kilimanjaro | [kilimɑn'dʂɑrʊ] |

129. Rivers

river	elv (m/f)	['ɛlv]
spring (natural source)	kilde (m)	['çildə]
riverbed (river channel)	elveleie (n)	['ɛlvəˌlæje]
basin (river valley)	flodbasseng (n)	['flʊd bɑˌseŋ]
to flow into ...	å munne ut ...	[ɔ 'mʉnə ʉt ...]

| tributary | bielv (m/f) | ['biˌelv] |
| bank (of river) | bredd (m) | ['brɛd] |

current (stream)	strøm (m)	['strøm]
downstream (adv)	medstrøms	['meˌstrøms]
upstream (adv)	motstrøms	['mʊtˌstrøms]

inundation	oversvømmelse (m)	['ɔvəˌsvœmelsə]
flooding	flom (m)	['flɔm]
to overflow (vi)	å overflø	[ɔ 'ɔvərˌflø]
to flood (vt)	å oversvømme	[ɔ 'ɔvəˌsvœmə]

| shallow (shoal) | grunne (m/f) | ['grʉnə] |
| rapids | stryk (m/n) | ['stryk] |

dam	demning (m)	['dɛmniŋ]
canal	kanal (m)	[kɑ'nɑl]
reservoir (artificial lake)	reservoar (n)	[resɛrvʊ'ɑr]
sluice, lock	sluse (m)	['ʂlʉsə]
water body (pond, etc.)	vannmasse (m)	['vɑnˌmɑsə]

swamp (marshland)	**myr, sump** (m)	['myr], ['sʉmp]
bog, marsh	**hengemyr** (m)	['hɛŋeˌmyr]
whirlpool	**virvel** (m)	['virvəl]
stream (brook)	**bekk** (m)	['bɛk]
drinking (ab. water)	**drikke-**	['drikə-]
fresh (~ water)	**fersk-**	['fæʂk-]
ice	**is** (m)	['is]
to freeze over (ab. river, etc.)	**å fryse til**	[ɔ 'frysə til]

130. Rivers names

Seine	**Seine**	['sɛːn]
Loire	**Loire**	[lu'ɑːr]
Thames	**Themsen**	['tɛmsən]
Rhine	**Rhinen**	['riːnən]
Danube	**Donau**	['dɔnaʉ]
Volga	**Volga**	['vɔlga]
Don	**Don**	['dɔn]
Lena	**Lena**	['lena]
Yellow River	**Huang He**	[ˌhwɑn'hɛ]
Yangtze	**Yangtze**	['jaŋtse]
Mekong	**Mekong**	[me'kɔŋ]
Ganges	**Ganges**	['gaŋes]
Nile River	**Nilen**	['nilən]
Congo River	**Kongo**	['kɔngʉ]
Okavango River	**Okavango**	[ʉka'vangʉ]
Zambezi River	**Zambezi**	[sam'besi]
Limpopo River	**Limpopo**	[limpɔ'pɔ]
Mississippi River	**Mississippi**	['misi'sipi]

131. Forest

forest, wood	**skog** (m)	['skʉg]
forest (as adj)	**skog-**	['skʉg-]
thick forest	**tett skog** (n)	['tɛt ˌskʉg]
grove	**lund** (m)	['lʉn]
forest clearing	**glenne** (m/f)	['glenə]
thicket	**krattskog** (m)	['kratˌskʉg]
scrubland	**kratt** (n)	['krat]
footpath (troddenpath)	**sti** (m)	['sti]
gully	**ravine** (m)	[ra'vinə]
tree	**tre** (n)	['trɛ]
leaf	**blad** (n)	['blɑ]

leaves (foliage)	løv (n)	['løv]
fall of leaves	løvfall (n)	['løv‚fɑl]
to fall (ab. leaves)	å falle	[ɔ 'fɑlə]
top (of the tree)	tretopp (m)	['trɛ‚tɔp]

branch	kvist, gren (m)	['kvist], ['gren]
bough	gren, grein (m/f)	['gren], ['græjn]
bud (on shrub, tree)	knopp (m)	['knɔp]
needle (of pine tree)	nål (m/f)	['nɔl]
fir cone	kongle (m/f)	['kʊŋlə]

hollow (in a tree)	trehull (n)	['trɛ‚hʉl]
nest	reir (n)	['ræjr]
burrow (animal hole)	hule (m/f)	['hʉlə]

trunk	stamme (m)	['stɑmə]
root	rot (m/f)	['rʊt]
bark	bark (m)	['bɑrk]
moss	mose (m)	['mʊsə]

to uproot (remove trees or tree stumps)	å rykke opp med roten	[ɔ 'rʏkə ɔp me 'rutən]
to chop down	å felle	[ɔ 'fɛlə]
to deforest (vt)	å hogge ned	[ɔ 'hɔgə 'ne]
tree stump	stubbe (m)	['stʉbə]

campfire	bål (n)	['bɔl]
forest fire	skogbrann (m)	['skʊg‚brɑn]
to extinguish (vt)	å slokke	[ɔ 'ʂløkə]

forest ranger	skogvokter (m)	['skʊg‚vɔktər]
protection	vern (n), beskyttelse (m)	['væːn], ['be'ʂytəlsə]
to protect (~ nature)	å beskytte	[ɔ be'ʂytə]
poacher	tyvskytter (m)	['tyf‚ʂytər]
steel trap	saks (m/f)	['sɑks]

| to gather, to pick (vt) | å plukke | [ɔ 'plʉkə] |
| to lose one's way | å gå seg vill | [ɔ 'gɔ sæj 'vil] |

132. Natural resources

natural resources	naturressurser (m pl)	[nɑ'tʉr rɛ'sʉsər]
minerals	mineraler (n pl)	[minə'rɑlər]
deposits	forekomster (m pl)	['forə‚kɔmstər]
field (e.g. oilfield)	felt (m)	['fɛlt]

to mine (extract)	å utvinne	[ɔ 'ʉt‚vinə]
mining (extraction)	utvinning (m/f)	['ʉt‚viniŋ]
ore	malm (m)	['mɑlm]
mine (e.g. for coal)	gruve (m/f)	['grʉvə]
shaft (mine ~)	gruvesjakt (m/f)	['grʉvə‚sɑkt]
miner	gruvearbeider (m)	['grʉvə'ar‚bæjdər]
gas (natural ~)	gass (m)	['gɑs]
gas pipeline	gassledning (m)	['gɑs‚ledniŋ]

oil (petroleum)	olje (m)	['ɔljə]
oil pipeline	oljeledning (m)	['ɔljə‚lednɪŋ]
oil well	oljebrønn (m)	['ɔljə‚brœn]
derrick (tower)	boretårn (n)	['boːrə‚tɔːn]
tanker	tankskip (n)	['tɑnk‚sip]

sand	sand (m)	['sɑn]
limestone	kalkstein (m)	['kɑlk‚stæjn]
gravel	grus (m)	['grʉs]
peat	torv (m/f)	['tɔrv]
clay	leir (n)	['læjr]
coal	kull (n)	['kʉl]

iron (ore)	jern (n)	['jæːn]
gold	gull (n)	['gʉl]
silver	sølv (n)	['søl]
nickel	nikkel (m)	['nikəl]
copper	kobber (n)	['kɔbər]

zinc	sink (m/n)	['sink]
manganese	mangan (m/n)	[mɑ'ŋɑn]
mercury	kvikksølv (n)	['kvik‚søl]
lead	bly (n)	['bly]

mineral	mineral (n)	[minə'rɑl]
crystal	krystall (m/n)	[kry'stɑl]
marble	marmor (m/n)	['mɑrmʉr]
uranium	uran (m/n)	[ʉ'rɑn]

The Earth. Part 2

133. Weather

weather	vær (n)	['vær]
weather forecast	værvarsel (n)	['vær̩ˌvɑʂəl]
temperature	temperatur (m)	[tɛmpərɑ'tʉr]
thermometer	termometer (n)	[tɛrmʉ'metər]
barometer	barometer (n)	[bɑrʉ'metər]
humid (adj)	fuktig	['fʉkti]
humidity	fuktighet (m)	['fʉktiˌhet]
heat (extreme ~)	hete (m)	['he:tə]
hot (torrid)	het	['het]
it's hot	det er hett	[de ær 'het]
it's warm	det er varmt	[de ær 'vɑrmt]
warm (moderately hot)	varm	['vɑrm]
it's cold	det er kaldt	[de ær 'kɑlt]
cold (adj)	kald	['kɑl]
sun	sol (m/f)	['sʉl]
to shine (vi)	å skinne	[ɔ 'ʂinə]
sunny (day)	solrik	['sʉlˌrik]
to come up (vi)	å gå opp	[ɔ 'gɔ ɔp]
to set (vi)	å gå ned	[ɔ 'gɔ ne]
cloud	sky (m)	['ʂy]
cloudy (adj)	skyet	['ʂy:ət]
rain cloud	regnsky (m/f)	['ræjnˌʂy]
somber (gloomy)	mørk	['mœrk]
rain	regn (n)	['ræjn]
it's raining	det regner	[de 'ræjnər]
rainy (~ day, weather)	regnværs-	['ræjnˌvæʂ-]
to drizzle (vi)	å småregne	[ɔ 'smo:ræjnə]
pouring rain	piskende regn (n)	['piskenə ˌræjn]
downpour	styrtregn (n)	['styːtˌræjn]
heavy (e.g. ~ rain)	kraftig, sterk	['krɑfti], ['stærk]
puddle	vannpytt (m)	['vɑnˌpyt]
to get wet (in rain)	å bli våt	[ɔ 'bli 'vot]
fog (mist)	tåke (m/f)	['to:kə]
foggy	tåke	['to:kə]
snow	snø (m)	['snø]
it's snowing	det snør	[de 'snør]

134. Severe weather. Natural disasters

thunderstorm	tordenvær (n)	['tʊrdən‚vær]
lightning (~ strike)	lyn (n)	['lyn]
to flash (vi)	å glimte	[ɔ 'glimtə]
thunder	torden (m)	['tʊrdən]
to thunder (vi)	å tordne	[ɔ 'tʊrdnə]
it's thundering	det tordner	[de 'tʊrdnər]
hail	hagle (m/f)	['haglə]
it's hailing	det hagler	[de 'haglər]
to flood (vt)	å oversvømme	[ɔ 'ɔvə‚svœmə]
flood, inundation	oversvømmelse (m)	['ɔvə‚svœmelsə]
earthquake	jordskjelv (n)	['juːr‚ʂɛlv]
tremor, quake	skjelv (n)	['ʂɛlv]
epicentre	episenter (n)	[ɛpi'sɛntər]
eruption	utbrudd (n)	['ʉt‚brʉd]
lava	lava (m)	['lava]
twister	skypumpe (m/f)	['sy‚pʉmpə]
tornado	tornado (m)	[tʊ:'ɳadʉ]
typhoon	tyfon (m)	[ty'fʊn]
hurricane	orkan (m)	[ɔr'kan]
storm	storm (m)	['stɔrm]
tsunami	tsunami (m)	[tsʉ'nami]
cyclone	syklon (m)	[sy'klun]
bad weather	uvær (n)	['ʉ:‚vær]
fire (accident)	brann (m)	['bran]
disaster	katastrofe (m)	[kata'strɔfə]
meteorite	meteoritt (m)	[meteʉ'rit]
avalanche	lavine (m)	[la'vinə]
snowslide	snøskred, snøras (n)	['snø‚skred], ['snøras]
blizzard	snøstorm (m)	['snø‚stɔrm]
snowstorm	snøstorm (m)	['snø‚stɔrm]

Fauna

135. Mammals. Predators

predator	rovdyr (n)	['rɔv,dyr]
tiger	tiger (m)	['tigər]
lion	løve (m/f)	['løve]
wolf	ulv (m)	['ʉlv]
fox	rev (m)	['rev]
jaguar	jaguar (m)	[jagʉ'ar]
leopard	leopard (m)	[leʊ'pard]
cheetah	gepard (m)	[ge'pard]
black panther	panter (m)	['pantər]
puma	puma (m)	['pʉma]
snow leopard	snøleopard (m)	['snø leʊ'pard]
lynx	gaupe (m/f)	['gaʊpə]
coyote	coyote, prærieulv (m)	[kɔ'jote], ['præri,ʉlv]
jackal	sjakal (m)	[ʂa'kal]
hyena	hyene (m)	[hy'ene]

136. Wild animals

animal	dyr (n)	['dyr]
beast (animal)	best, udyr (n)	['bɛst], ['ʉ,dyr]
squirrel	ekorn (n)	['ɛkʊ:ŋ]
hedgehog	pinnsvin (n)	['pin,svin]
hare	hare (m)	['harə]
rabbit	kanin (m)	[ka'nin]
badger	grevling (m)	['grɛvliŋ]
raccoon	vaskebjørn (m)	['vaskə,bjœ:ŋ]
hamster	hamster (m)	['hamstər]
marmot	murmeldyr (n)	['mʉrməl,dyr]
mole	muldvarp (m)	['mʉl,varp]
mouse	mus (m/f)	['mʉs]
rat	rotte (m/f)	['rɔtə]
bat	flaggermus (m/f)	['flagər,mʉs]
ermine	røyskatt (m)	['røjskat]
sable	sobel (m)	['sʊbəl]
marten	mår (m)	['mɔr]
weasel	snømus (m/f)	['snø,mʉs]
mink	mink (m)	['mink]

| beaver | bever (m) | ['bevər] |
| otter | oter (m) | ['ʊtər] |

horse	hest (m)	['hɛst]
moose	elg (m)	['ɛlg]
deer	hjort (m)	['jɔːt]
camel	kamel (m)	[ka'mel]

bison	bison (m)	['bisɔn]
aurochs	urokse (m)	['ʉrˌʊksə]
buffalo	bøffel (m)	['bøfəl]

zebra	sebra (m)	['sebra]
antelope	antilope (m)	[anti'lʊpə]
roe deer	rådyr (n)	['roˌdyr]
fallow deer	dåhjort, dådyr (n)	['dɔˌjɔː t], ['dɔˌdyr]
chamois	gemse (m)	['gɛmsə]
wild boar	villsvin (n)	['vilˌsvin]

whale	hval (m)	['val]
seal	sel (m)	['sel]
walrus	hvalross (m)	['valˌrɔs]
fur seal	pelssel (m)	['pɛlsˌsel]
dolphin	delfin (m)	[dɛl'fin]

bear	bjørn (m)	['bjœː ŋ]
polar bear	isbjørn (m)	['isˌbjœː ŋ]
panda	panda (m)	['panda]

monkey	ape (m/f)	['ape]
chimpanzee	sjimpanse (m)	[ʂim'pansə]
orangutan	orangutang (m)	[ʊ'rangʉˌtaŋ]
gorilla	gorilla (m)	[gɔ'rila]
macaque	makak (m)	[ma'kak]
gibbon	gibbon (m)	['gibʊn]

elephant	elefant (m)	[ɛle'fant]
rhinoceros	neshorn (n)	['nesˌhʊː ŋ]
giraffe	sjiraff (m)	[ʂi'raf]
hippopotamus	flodhest (m)	['flʊdˌhɛst]

| kangaroo | kenguru (m) | ['kɛŋgʉrʉ] |
| koala (bear) | koala (m) | [kʊ'ala] |

mongoose	mangust, mungo (m)	[maŋ'gʉst], ['mʉŋgu]
chinchilla	chinchilla (m)	[ʂin'ʂila]
skunk	skunk (m)	['skunk]
porcupine	hulepinnsvin (n)	['hʉləˌpinsvin]

137. Domestic animals

cat	katt (m)	['kat]
tomcat	hannkatt (m)	['hanˌkat]
dog	hund (m)	['hʉn]

horse	hest (m)	['hɛst]
stallion (male horse)	hingst (m)	['hiŋst]
mare	hoppe, merr (m/f)	['hɔpə], ['mɛr]

cow	ku (f)	['kʉ]
bull	tyr (m)	['tyr]
ox	okse (m)	['ɔksə]

sheep (ewe)	sau (m)	['saʉ]
ram	vær, saubukk (m)	['vær], ['saʉˌbʉk]
goat	geit (m/f)	['jæjt]
billy goat, he-goat	geitebukk (m)	['jæjtəˌbʉk]

| donkey | esel (n) | ['ɛsəl] |
| mule | muldyr (n) | ['mʉlˌdyr] |

pig	svin (n)	['svin]
piglet	gris (m)	['gris]
rabbit	kanin (m)	[kɑ'nin]

| hen (chicken) | høne (m/f) | ['hønə] |
| cock | hane (m) | ['hɑnə] |

duck	and (m/f)	['ɑn]
drake	andrik (m)	['ɑndrik]
goose	gås (m/f)	['gɔs]

| tom turkey, gobbler | kalkunhane (m) | [kɑl'kʉnˌhɑnə] |
| turkey (hen) | kalkunhøne (m/f) | [kɑl'kʉnˌhønə] |

domestic animals	husdyr (n pl)	['hʉsˌdyr]
tame (e.g. ~ hamster)	tam	['tɑm]
to tame (vt)	å temme	[ɔ 'tɛmə]
to breed (vt)	å avle, å oppdrette	[ɔ 'ɑvlə], [ɔ 'ɔpˌdrɛtə]

farm	farm, gård (m)	['fɑrm], ['gɔːr]
poultry	fjærfe (n)	['fjærˌfɛ]
cattle	kveg (n)	['kvɛg]
herd (cattle)	flokk, bøling (m)	['flɔk], ['bøliŋ]

stable	stall (m)	['stɑl]
pigsty	grisehus (n)	['grisəˌhʉs]
cowshed	kufjøs (m/n)	['kuˌfjøs]
rabbit hutch	kaninbur (n)	[kɑ'ninˌbʉr]
hen house	hønsehus (n)	['hønsəˌhʉs]

138. Birds

bird	fugl (m)	['fʉl]
pigeon	due (m/f)	['dʉə]
sparrow	spurv (m)	['spʉrv]
tit (great tit)	kjøttmeis (m/f)	['çœtˌmæjs]
magpie	skjære (m/f)	['şærə]
raven	ravn (m)	['rɑvn]

crow	**kråke** (m)	['kro:kə]
jackdaw	**kaie** (m/f)	['kɑjə]
rook	**kornkråke** (m/f)	['kʊːnˌkro:kə]
duck	**and** (m/f)	['ɑn]
goose	**gås** (m/f)	['gɔs]
pheasant	**fasan** (m)	[fɑ'sɑn]
eagle	**ørn** (m/f)	['œ:ɳ]
hawk	**hauk** (m)	['haʊk]
falcon	**falk** (m)	['fɑlk]
vulture	**gribb** (m)	['grib]
condor (Andean ~)	**kondor** (m)	[kʊn'dʊr]
swan	**svane** (m/f)	['svɑnə]
crane	**trane** (m/f)	['trɑnə]
stork	**stork** (m)	['stɔrk]
parrot	**papegøye** (m)	[pɑpe'gøjə]
hummingbird	**kolibri** (m)	[kʊ'libri]
peacock	**påfugl** (m)	['pɔˌfʉl]
ostrich	**struts** (m)	['strʉts]
heron	**hegre** (m)	['hæjrə]
flamingo	**flamingo** (m)	[flɑ'mingʊ]
pelican	**pelikan** (m)	[peli'kɑn]
nightingale	**nattergal** (m)	['nɑtərˌgɑl]
swallow	**svale** (m/f)	['svɑlə]
thrush	**trost** (m)	['trʊst]
song thrush	**måltrost** (m)	['mo:lˌtrʊst]
blackbird	**svarttrost** (m)	['svɑːˌtrʊst]
swift	**tårnseiler** (m), **tårnsvale** (m/f)	['tɔːɳˌsæjlə], ['tɔːɳˌsvɑlə]
lark	**lerke** (m/f)	['lærkə]
quail	**vaktel** (m)	['vɑktəl]
woodpecker	**hakkespett** (m)	['hɑkəˌspɛt]
cuckoo	**gjøk, gauk** (m)	['jøk], ['gaʊk]
owl	**ugle** (m/f)	['ʉglə]
eagle owl	**hubro** (m)	['hʉbrʊ]
wood grouse	**storfugl** (m)	['stʊrˌfʉl]
black grouse	**orrfugl** (m)	['ɔrˌfʉl]
partridge	**rapphøne** (m/f)	['rɑpˌhønə]
starling	**stær** (m)	['stær]
canary	**kanarifugl** (m)	[kɑ'nɑriˌfʉl]
hazel grouse	**jerpe** (m/f)	['jærpə]
chaffinch	**bokfink** (m)	['bʊkˌfink]
bullfinch	**dompap** (m)	['dʊmpɑp]
seagull	**måke** (m/f)	['mo:kə]
albatross	**albatross** (m)	['ɑlbɑˌtrɔs]
penguin	**pingvin** (m)	[piŋ'vin]

139. Fish. Marine animals

bream	brasme (m/f)	['brɑsmə]
carp	karpe (m)	['kɑrpə]
perch	åbor (m)	['obɔr]
catfish	malle (m)	['mɑlə]
pike	gjedde (m/f)	['jɛdə]

| salmon | laks (m) | ['lɑks] |
| sturgeon | stør (m) | ['stør] |

herring	sild (m/f)	['sil]
Atlantic salmon	atlanterhavslaks (m)	[at'lɑntərhɑfs,lɑks]
mackerel	makrell (m)	[mɑ'krɛl]
flatfish	rødspette (m/f)	['rø,spɛtə]

zander, pike perch	gjørs (m)	['jøːʂ]
cod	torsk (m)	['tɔʂk]
tuna	tunfisk (m)	['tʉn,fisk]
trout	ørret (m)	['øret]

eel	ål (m)	['ɔl]
electric ray	elektrisk rokke (m/f)	[ɛ'lektrisk ,rɔkə]
moray eel	murene (m)	[mʉ'rɛnə]
piranha	piraja (m)	[pi'rɑja]

shark	hai (m)	['hɑj]
dolphin	delfin (m)	[dɛl'fin]
whale	hval (m)	['vɑl]

crab	krabbe (m)	['krɑbə]
jellyfish	manet (m/f), meduse (m)	['mɑnet], [me'dʉsə]
octopus	blekksprut (m)	['blek,sprʉt]

starfish	sjøstjerne (m/f)	['ʂø,stjæːɳə]
sea urchin	sjøpinnsvin (n)	['ʂøː'pin,svin]
seahorse	sjøhest (m)	['ʂø,hɛst]

oyster	østers (m)	['østəʂ]
prawn	reke (m/f)	['rekə]
lobster	hummer (m)	['hʉmər]
spiny lobster	langust (m)	[lɑŋ'gʉst]

140. Amphibians. Reptiles

| snake | slange (m) | ['ʂlɑŋə] |
| venomous (snake) | giftig | ['jifti] |

viper	hoggorm, huggorm (m)	['hʊg,ɔrm], ['hʉg,ɔrm]
cobra	kobra (m)	['kʊbrɑ]
python	pyton (m)	['pytɔn]
boa	boaslange (m)	['bɔɑ,slɑŋə]
grass snake	snok (m)	['snʊk]

| rattle snake | klapperslange (m) | ['klapə‚slaŋə] |
| anaconda | anakonda (m) | [ana'kɔnda] |

lizard	øgle (m/f)	['øglə]
iguana	iguan (m)	[igʉ'an]
monitor lizard	varan (n)	[va'ran]
salamander	salamander (m)	[sala'mandər]
chameleon	kameleon (m)	[kaməle'ʉn]
scorpion	skorpion (m)	[skɔrpi'ʉn]

turtle	skilpadde (m/f)	['ʂil‚padə]
frog	frosk (m)	['frɔsk]
toad	padde (m/f)	['padə]
crocodile	krokodille (m)	[krʊkə'dilə]

141. Insects

insect	insekt (n)	['insɛkt]
butterfly	sommerfugl (m)	['sɔmər‚fʉl]
ant	maur (m)	['maʊr]
fly	flue (m/f)	['flʉə]
mosquito	mygg (m)	['mʏg]
beetle	bille (m)	['bilə]

wasp	veps (m)	['vɛps]
bee	bie (m/f)	['biə]
bumblebee	humle (m/f)	['hʉmlə]
gadfly (botfly)	brems (m)	['brɛms]

| spider | edderkopp (m) | ['ɛdər‚kɔp] |
| spider's web | edderkoppnett (n) | ['ɛdərkɔp‚nɛt] |

dragonfly	øyenstikker (m)	['øjən‚stikər]
grasshopper	gresshoppe (m/f)	['grɛs‚hɔpə]
moth (night butterfly)	nattsvermer (m)	['nat‚sværmər]

cockroach	kakerlakk (m)	[kakə'lak]
tick	flått, midd (m)	['flɔt], ['mid]
flea	loppe (f)	['lɔpə]
midge	knott (m)	['knɔt]

locust	vandgresshoppe (m/f)	['van 'grɛs‚hɔpə]
snail	snegl (m)	['snæjl]
cricket	siriss (m)	['si‚ris]
firefly	ildflue (m/f), lysbille (m)	['il‚flʉə], ['lys‚bilə]
ladybird	marihøne (m/f)	['mari‚hønə]
cockchafer	oldenborre (f)	['ɔldən‚bɔrə]

leech	igle (m/f)	['iglə]
caterpillar	sommerfugllarve (m/f)	['sɔmərfʉl‚larvə]
earthworm	meitemark (m)	['mæjtə‚mark]
larva	larve (m/f)	['larvə]

Flora

142. Trees

tree	tre (n)	['trɛ]
deciduous (adj)	løv-	['løv-]
coniferous (adj)	bar-	['bɑr-]
evergreen (adj)	eviggrønt	['ɛvi̩grœnt]
apple tree	epletre (n)	['ɛplə̩trɛ]
pear tree	pæretre (n)	['pærə̩trɛ]
sweet cherry tree	morelltre (n)	[mʉ'rɛl̩trɛ]
sour cherry tree	kirsebærtre (n)	['çisəbær̩trɛ]
plum tree	plommetre (n)	['plʉmə̩trɛ]
birch	bjørk (f)	['bjœrk]
oak	eik (f)	['æjk]
linden tree	lind (m/f)	['lin]
aspen	osp (m/f)	['ɔsp]
maple	lønn (m/f)	['lœn]
spruce	gran (m/f)	['grɑn]
pine	furu (m/f)	['fʉrʉ]
larch	lerk (m)	['lærk]
fir tree	edelgran (m/f)	['ɛdəl̩grɑn]
cedar	seder (m)	['sedər]
poplar	poppel (m)	['pɔpəl]
rowan	rogn (m/f)	['rɔŋn]
willow	pil (m/f)	['pil]
alder	or, older (m/f)	['ʉr], ['ɔldər]
beech	bøk (m)	['bøk]
elm	alm (m)	['ɑlm]
ash (tree)	ask (m/f)	['ɑsk]
chestnut	kastanjetre (n)	[kɑ'stɑnje̩trɛ]
magnolia	magnolia (m)	[mɑŋ'nʉliɑ]
palm tree	palme (m)	['pɑlmə]
cypress	sypress (m)	[sʏ'prɛs]
mangrove	mangrove (m)	[mɑŋ'grʉvə]
baobab	apebrødtre (n)	['ɑpebrø̩trɛ]
eucalyptus	eukalyptus (m)	[ɛvkɑ'lyptʉs]
sequoia	sequoia (m)	['sek̩vɔjɑ]

143. Shrubs

bush	busk (m)	['bʉsk]
shrub	busk (m)	['bʉsk]

| grapevine | vinranke (m) | ['vin‚rankə] |
| vineyard | vinmark (m/f) | ['vin‚mark] |

raspberry bush	bringebærbusk (m)	['briŋə‚bær busk]
blackcurrant bush	solbærbusk (m)	['sulbær‚busk]
redcurrant bush	ripsbusk (m)	['rips‚busk]
gooseberry bush	stikkelsbærbusk (m)	['stikəlsbær‚busk]

acacia	akasie (m)	[a'kasiə]
barberry	berberis (m)	['bærberis]
jasmine	sjasmin (m)	[ʂas'min]

juniper	einer (m)	['æjnər]
rosebush	rosenbusk (m)	['rusən‚busk]
dog rose	steinnype (m/f)	['stæjn‚nypə]

144. Fruits. Berries

fruit	frukt (m/f)	['frukt]
fruits	frukter (m/f pl)	['fruktər]
apple	eple (n)	['ɛplə]
pear	pære (m/f)	['pærə]
plum	plomme (m/f)	['plumə]

strawberry (garden ~)	jordbær (n)	['ju:r‚bær]
sour cherry	kirsebær (n)	['çiʂə‚bær]
sweet cherry	morell (m)	[mu'rɛl]
grape	drue (m)	['druə]

raspberry	bringebær (n)	['briŋə‚bær]
blackcurrant	solbær (n)	['sul‚bær]
redcurrant	rips (m)	['rips]
gooseberry	stikkelsbær (n)	['stikəls‚bær]
cranberry	tranebær (n)	['tranə‚bær]

orange	appelsin (m)	[apel'sin]
tangerine	mandarin (m)	[manda'rin]
pineapple	ananas (m)	['ananas]

| banana | banan (m) | [ba'nan] |
| date | daddel (m) | ['dadəl] |

lemon	sitron (m)	[si'trun]
apricot	aprikos (m)	[apri'kus]
peach	fersken (m)	['fæʂkən]

| kiwi | kiwi (m) | ['kivi] |
| grapefruit | grapefrukt (m/f) | ['grɛjp‚frukt] |

berry	bær (n)	['bær]
berries	bær (n pl)	['bær]
cowberry	tyttebær (n)	['tʏtə‚bær]
wild strawberry	markjordbær (n)	['mark ju:r‚bær]
bilberry	blåbær (n)	['blɔ‚bær]

145. Flowers. Plants

flower	blomst (m)	['blɔmst]
bouquet (of flowers)	bukett (m)	[bʉ'kɛt]
rose (flower)	rose (m/f)	['rʉsə]
tulip	tulipan (m)	[tʉli'pɑn]
carnation	nellik (m)	['nɛlik]
gladiolus	gladiolus (m)	[glɑdi'ɔlʉs]
cornflower	kornblomst (m)	['kʉːˌn̩blɔmst]
harebell	blåklokke (m/f)	['blɔˌklɔkə]
dandelion	løvetann (m/f)	['løvəˌtɑn]
camomile	kamille (m)	[kɑ'milə]
aloe	aloe (m)	['ɑlʉe]
cactus	kaktus (m)	['kɑktʉs]
rubber plant, ficus	gummiplante (m/f)	['gʉmiˌplɑntə]
lily	lilje (m)	['liljə]
geranium	geranium (m)	[ge'rɑnium]
hyacinth	hyasint (m)	[hiɑ'sint]
mimosa	mimose (m/f)	[mi'mɔsə]
narcissus	narsiss (m)	[nɑ'ʂis]
nasturtium	blomkarse (m)	['blɔmˌkɑʂə]
orchid	orkidé (m)	[ɔrki'de]
peony	peon, pion (m)	[pe'ʊn], [pi'ʊn]
violet	fiol (m)	[fi'ʊl]
pansy	stemorsblomst (m)	['stemʊʂˌblɔmst]
forget-me-not	forglemmegei (m)	[fɔr'gleməjæj]
daisy	tusenfryd (m)	['tʉsənˌfryd]
poppy	valmue (m)	['vɑlmʉe]
hemp	hamp (m)	['hɑmp]
mint	mynte (m/f)	['mʏntə]
lily of the valley	liljekonvall (m)	['liljə kɔn'vɑl]
snowdrop	snøklokke (m/f)	['snøˌklɔkə]
nettle	nesle (m/f)	['nɛslə]
sorrel	syre (m/f)	['syrə]
water lily	nøkkerose (m/f)	['nøkəˌrʉse]
fern	bregne (m/f)	['brɛjnə]
lichen	lav (m/n)	['lɑv]
greenhouse (tropical ~)	drivhus (n)	['drivˌhʉs]
lawn	gressplen (m)	['grɛsˌplen]
flowerbed	blomsterbed (n)	['blɔmstərˌbed]
plant	plante (m/f), vekst (m)	['plɑntə], ['vɛkst]
grass	gras (n)	['grɑs]
blade of grass	grasstrå (n)	['grɑsˌstrɔ]

leaf	blad (n)	['blɑ]
petal	kronblad (n)	['krɔnˌblɑ]
stem	stilk (m)	['stilk]
tuber	rotknoll (m)	['rʊtˌknɔl]

| young plant (shoot) | spire (m/f) | ['spirə] |
| thorn | torn (m) | ['tʊːɳ] |

to blossom (vi)	å blomstre	[ɔ 'blɔmstrə]
to fade, to wither	å visne	[ɔ 'visnə]
smell (odour)	lukt (m/f)	['lʉkt]
to cut (flowers)	å skjære av	[ɔ 'ʂæːrə ɑː]
to pick (a flower)	å plukke	[ɔ 'plʉkə]

146. Cereals, grains

grain	korn (n)	['kʊːɳ]
cereal crops	cerealer (n pl)	[sere'ɑlər]
ear (of barley, etc.)	aks (n)	['ɑks]

wheat	hvete (m)	['vetə]
rye	rug (m)	['rʉg]
oats	havre (m)	['hɑvrə]
millet	hirse (m)	['hiʂə]
barley	bygg (m/n)	['bʏg]

maize	mais (m)	['mɑis]
rice	ris (m)	['ris]
buckwheat	bokhvete (m)	['bʊkˌvetə]

pea plant	ert (m/f)	['æːt]
kidney bean	bønne (m/f)	['bœnə]
soya	soya (m)	['sɔja]
lentil	linse (m/f)	['linsə]
beans (pulse crops)	bønner (m/f pl)	['bœnər]

COUNTRIES. NATIONALITIES

147. Western Europe

Europe	Europa	[ɛʉ'rʊpɑ]
European Union	Den Europeiske Union	[den ɛʉrʊ'pɛiskə ʉni'ɔn]
Austria	Østerrike	['østə͵rikə]
Great Britain	Storbritannia	['stʉr bri͵tɑniɑ]
England	England	['ɛŋlɑn]
Belgium	Belgia	['bɛlgiɑ]
Germany	Tyskland	['tʏsklɑn]
Netherlands	Nederland	['nedə͵lɑn]
Holland	Holland	['hɔlɑn]
Greece	Hellas	['hɛlɑs]
Denmark	Danmark	['dɑnmɑrk]
Ireland	Irland	['irlɑn]
Iceland	Island	['islɑn]
Spain	Spania	['spɑniɑ]
Italy	Italia	[i'tɑliɑ]
Cyprus	Kypros	['kʏprʊs]
Malta	Malta	['mɑltɑ]
Norway	Norge	['nɔrgə]
Portugal	Portugal	[pɔːʈʉ'gɑl]
Finland	Finland	['finlɑn]
France	Frankrike	['frɑnkrikə]
Sweden	Sverige	['sværiə]
Switzerland	Sveits	['svæjts]
Scotland	Skottland	['skɔtlɑn]
Vatican	Vatikanet	['vɑti͵kɑne]
Liechtenstein	Liechtenstein	['lihtɛnʂtæjn]
Luxembourg	Luxembourg	['lʉksɛm͵bʉrg]
Monaco	Monaco	[mʊ'nɑkʊ]

148. Central and Eastern Europe

Albania	Albania	[al'bɑniɑ]
Bulgaria	Bulgaria	[bʉl'gɑriɑ]
Hungary	Ungarn	['ʉŋɑːŋ]
Latvia	Latvia	['lɑtviɑ]
Lithuania	Litauen	['li͵tɑʊən]
Poland	Polen	['pʊlen]

Romania	Romania	[rʊ'mɑnia]
Serbia	Serbia	['særbia]
Slovakia	Slovakia	[ʂlʊ'vakia]

Croatia	Kroatia	[krʊ'ɑtia]
Czech Republic	Tsjekkia	['tʂɛkija]
Estonia	Estland	['ɛstlɑn]

Bosnia and Herzegovina	Bosnia-Hercegovina	['bɔsnia hersegɔ,vina]
Macedonia (Republic of ~)	Makedonia	[make'dɔnia]
Slovenia	Slovenia	[ʂlʊ'venia]
Montenegro	Montenegro	['mɔntə,nɛgrʊ]

149. Former USSR countries

| Azerbaijan | Aserbajdsjan | [ɑserbɑjd'ʂɑn] |
| Armenia | Armenia | [ar'menia] |

Belarus	Hviterussland	['vitə,rʉslɑn]
Georgia	Georgia	[ge'ɔrgia]
Kazakhstan	Kasakhstan	[ka'sak,stɑn]
Kirghizia	Kirgisistan	[kir'gisi,stɑn]
Moldova, Moldavia	Moldova	[mɔl'dɔva]

| Russia | Russland | ['rʉslɑn] |
| Ukraine | Ukraina | [ʉkra'ina] |

Tajikistan	Tadsjikistan	[ta'dʂiki,stɑn]
Turkmenistan	Turkmenistan	[tʉrk'meni,stɑn]
Uzbekistan	Usbekistan	[ʉs'beki,stɑn]

150. Asia

Asia	Asia	['ɑsia]
Vietnam	Vietnam	['vjɛtnɑm]
India	India	['india]
Israel	Israel	['israəl]

China	Kina	['çina]
Lebanon	Libanon	['libanɔn]
Mongolia	Mongolia	[mʊŋ'gulia]

| Malaysia | Malaysia | [ma'lajsia] |
| Pakistan | Pakistan | ['paki,stɑn] |

Saudi Arabia	Saudi-Arabia	['saʊdi a'rabia]
Thailand	Thailand	['tajlɑn]
Taiwan	Taiwan	['taj,van]
Turkey	Tyrkia	[tyrkia]
Japan	Japan	['japɑn]
Afghanistan	Afghanistan	[af'gani,stɑn]
Bangladesh	Bangladesh	[bangla'dɛʂ]

| Indonesia | Indonesia | [indʉˈnesia] |
| Jordan | Jordan | [ˈjɔrdan] |

| Iraq | Irak | [ˈirak] |
| Iran | Iran | [ˈiran] |

| Cambodia | Kambodsja | [kamˈbɔdşa] |
| Kuwait | Kuwait | [ˈkʉvajt] |

Laos	Laos	[ˈlaɔs]
Myanmar	Myanmar	[ˈmjænma]
Nepal	Nepal	[ˈnepal]
United Arab Emirates	Forente Arabiske Emiratene	[fɔˈrentə aˈrabiskə ɛmiˈratenə]

| Syria | Syria | [ˈsyria] |
| Palestine | Palestina | [paleˈstina] |

| South Korea | Sør-Korea | [ˈsør kʉˌrea] |
| North Korea | Nord-Korea | [ˈnuːr kʉˈrɛa] |

151. North America

United States of America	Amerikas Forente Stater	[aˈmerikas fɔˈrɛntə ˈstatər]
Canada	Canada	[ˈkanada]
Mexico	Mexico	[ˈmɛksikʉ]

152. Central and South America

Argentina	Argentina	[argɛnˈtina]
Brazil	Brasilia	[braˈsilia]
Colombia	Colombia	[kɔˈlʉmbia]

| Cuba | Cuba | [ˈkʉba] |
| Chile | Chile | [ˈtşilə] |

| Bolivia | Bolivia | [bɔˈlivia] |
| Venezuela | Venezuela | [venesʉˈɛla] |

| Paraguay | Paraguay | [paragˈwaj] |
| Peru | Peru | [peˈruː] |

Suriname	Surinam	[ˈsʉriˌnam]
Uruguay	Uruguay	[ʉrygʉˈaj]
Ecuador	Ecuador	[ɛkʉaˈdɔr]

| The Bahamas | Bahamas | [baˈhamas] |
| Haiti | Haiti | [haˈiti] |

Dominican Republic	Dominikanske Republikken	[dʉminiˈkanskə repʉˈblikən]
Panama	Panama	[ˈpanama]
Jamaica	Jamaica	[şaˈmajka]

153. Africa

Egypt	Egypt	[ε'gypt]
Morocco	Marokko	[mɑ'rɔkʉ]
Tunisia	Tunisia	['tʉ'nisiɑ]
Ghana	Ghana	['gɑnɑ]
Zanzibar	Zanzibar	['sɑnsibɑr]
Kenya	Kenya	['kenyɑ]
Libya	Libya	['libiɑ]
Madagascar	Madagaskar	[mɑdɑ'gɑskɑr]
Namibia	Namibia	[nɑ'mibiɑ]
Senegal	Senegal	[sene'gɑl]
Tanzania	Tanzania	['tɑnsɑˌniɑ]
South Africa	Republikken Sør-Afrika	[repʉ'bliken 'sørˌɑfrikɑ]

154. Australia. Oceania

Australia	Australia	[aʊ'strɑliɑ]
New Zealand	New Zealand	[njʉ'selɑn]
Tasmania	Tasmania	[tɑs'mɑniɑ]
French Polynesia	Fransk Polynesia	['frɑnsk pɔly'nesiɑ]

155. Cities

Amsterdam	Amsterdam	['ɑmstɛrˌdɑm]
Ankara	Ankara	['ɑnkɑrɑ]
Athens	Athen, Aten	[ɑ'ten]
Baghdad	Bagdad	['bɑgdɑd]
Bangkok	Bangkok	['bɑnkɔk]
Barcelona	Barcelona	[bɑrsə'lunɑ]
Beijing	Peking, Beijing	['pekiŋ], ['bɛjʒin]
Beirut	Beirut	['bæjˌrʉt]
Berlin	Berlin	[bɛr'lin]
Mumbai (Bombay)	Bombay	['bɔmbɛj]
Bonn	Bonn	['bɔn]
Bordeaux	Bordeaux	[bɔr'dɔː]
Bratislava	Bratislava	[brɑti'slɑvɑ]
Brussels	Brussel	['brʉsɛl]
Bucharest	Bukarest	['bʉkɑ'rɛst]
Budapest	Budapest	['bʉdɑpɛst]
Cairo	Kairo	['kɑjrʉ]
Kolkata (Calcutta)	Calcutta	[kɑl'kʉtɑ]
Chicago	Chicago	[ʂi'kɑgʉ]
Copenhagen	København	['çøbənˌhɑvn]
Dar-es-Salaam	Dar-es-Salaam	['dɑresɑˌlɑm]

Delhi	Delhi	['dɛli]
Dubai	Dubai	['dɵbɑj]
Dublin	Dublin	['døblin]
Düsseldorf	Düsseldorf	['dɵsəlˌdɔrf]

Florence	Firenze	[fi'rɛnsə]
Frankfurt	Frankfurt	['frɑnkfɵːt]
Geneva	Genève	[ʂe'nɛv]

The Hague	Haag	['hɑg]
Hamburg	Hamburg	['hɑmbɵrg]
Hanoi	Hanoi	['hɑnɔj]
Havana	Havana	[hɑ'vɑnɑ]
Helsinki	Helsinki	['hɛlsinki]
Hiroshima	Hiroshima	[hirɵ'ʂimɑ]
Hong Kong	Hongkong	['hɔnˌkɔŋ]

Istanbul	Istanbul	['istɑnbɵl]
Jerusalem	Jerusalem	[je'rɵsɑlem]
Kyiv	Kiev	['kiːef]
Kuala Lumpur	Kuala Lumpur	[kɵ'ɑlɑ 'lɵmpɵr]
Lisbon	Lisboa	['lisbɵɑ]
London	London	['lɔndɔn]
Los Angeles	Los Angeles	[ˌlɔs'ændʒələs]
Lyons	Lyon	[li'ɔn]

Madrid	Madrid	[mɑ'drid]
Marseille	Marseille	[mɑr'sɛj]
Mexico City	Mexico City	['mɛksikɵ 'siti]
Miami	Miami	[mɑ'jami]
Montreal	Montreal	[mɔntri'ɔl]
Moscow	Moskva	[mɔ'skvɑ]
Munich	München	['mɵnhən]

Nairobi	Nairobi	[nɑj'rɵbi]
Naples	Napoli	['nɑpɵli]
New York	New York	[njɵ 'jork]
Nice	Nice	['nis]
Oslo	Oslo	['ɔʂlɵ]
Ottawa	Ottawa	['ɔtɑvɑ]

Paris	Paris	[pɑ'ris]
Prague	Praha	['prɑhɑ]
Rio de Janeiro	Rio de Janeiro	['riu de ʂɑ'næjrɵ]
Rome	Roma	['rɵmɑ]

Saint Petersburg	Sankt Petersburg	[ˌsɑnkt 'petɛ̌ʂˌbɵrg]
Seoul	Seoul	[se'uːl]
Shanghai	Shanghai	['ʂɑŋhɑj]
Singapore	Singapore	['siŋɑ'pɔr]
Stockholm	Stockholm	['stɔkhɔlm]
Sydney	Sydney	['sidni]

Taipei	Taipei	['tɑjpæj]
Tokyo	Tokyo	['tɔkiɵ]
Toronto	Toronto	[tɔ'rɔntɵ]

Venice	**Venezia**	[ve'netsia]
Vienna	**Wien**	['vin]
Warsaw	**Warszawa**	[va'ṣava]
Washington	**Washington**	['vɔṣiŋtən]

www.ingramcontent.com/pod-product-compliance
Lightning Source LLC
Chambersburg PA
CBHW070553050426

42450CB00011B/2850